Ranches of Isolation:

Transatlantic Poetry

Sally Connolly

MadHat Press
Asheville, North Carolina

MadHat Press
MadHat Incorporated
PO Box 8364, Asheville, NC 28814

Copyright © 2018 Sally Connolly
All rights reserved

The Library of Congress has assigned
this edition a Control Number of
2018959077

ISBN 978-1-941196-79-3 (paperback)

Cover art and design by Marc Vincenz
Book design by MadHat Press

www.madhat-press.com

First Printing

For Jordan J. Evans, my transatlantic muse

Table of Contents

Introduction: Meanwhile, Back at the Ranch ...   vii

I. THE OBSTINATE ISLES REVISITED

Explainers, Idiots and Laureates   3
"Breaking Bread with the Dead": W. H. Auden, Seamus Heaney,
 and Yeats's legacy   13

II. THE T. S. ELIOT PRIZE

The T. S. Eliot Prize in Poetry   43

III. TRANSATLANTIC TRAFFIC

Poems about Ezra Pound in Old Age   91
Two Interviews On Thom Gunn   100

IV. *AU CONTRAIRE:* THE CONDITION OF THE IRISH-ENGLISH

The Irish-English   135
An A—Z of Seamus Heaney   151
Two Genealogical Elegies for Seamus Heaney   160

V. SO LARGE, SO FRIENDLY AND SO RICH: ADVENTURES IN AMERICA

"A very deep rabbit": Strategies of Evasion and Obliquity
 in Susan Howe's "Thorow"   175
The poetry of 9/11: Keeping Yes and No Unsplit
 in the Dialectic of Disaster   182
The offspring of Ezra Pound's pact?
 Mark Doty's "Letter to Walt Whitman"   190

Acknowledgments   200
About the Author   203

Introduction:
Meanwhile, Back at the Ranch ...

Transatlanticism is a rather quaint notion. Outmoded, even. The transatlantic traffic between the UK and American that defined twentieth-century poetics—the figures of T. S. Eliot and W. H. Auden straddling the Atlantic like twin Colossi of Rhodes—has, quite rightly, given way to a twenty-first-century transnationalism. The approach allows for a far more diverse and inclusive understanding of literatures in English beyond those boundaries delineated by the canonical dead white dudes of the twentieth-century Anglo-American "tradition."

As retrograde as it may be, then, my entire adult life has been defined by transatlantic poetics; which is quite an assertion considering that I didn't even know that American poetry existed until I was sixteen. Certainly poetry didn't feature at all in my home life; neither of my parents (both of whom left school at fourteen without a qualification between them) had any interest whatsoever in poetry. Though formally uneducated, my father had a love of, and rabid hunger for, books that is often found in autodidacts. He still has the well-thumbed and dog-eared copy of T. E. Lawrence's *The Seven Pillars of Wisdom* that accompanied him on one of his sojourns "detained at her Majesty's Pleasure" as they quaintly and euphemistically have it in the UK. Poetry, though not so much.

My first encounters with verse came at Lyndale School in St Albans, England, in the early 1980s. This was an extraordinarily unorthodox educational institution along the lines of the British cartoonist Ronald Searle's fictional and madcap St Trinian's. Certainly the uniforms, straight out of the British prep-school playbook—box-pleat gym tunics, sashes, straw boaters—were almost entirely identical. The curriculum followed no known or recommended educational program and was wholly informed by the likes and dislikes of our headmistress, the formidable septuagenarian Mrs. Biddy Hodge. Consequently, my early education mainly consisted of field hockey, the study of fossils and the works of Alfred, Lord Tennyson. Mrs. Hodge's father, the schoolmaster and amateur paleontologist Frank Mozart Walker, had met the great poet of the Victorian era while holidaying in the late 1880s at the family's home in Seaview on the Isle of Wight where Tennyson also regularly vacationed. The Isle of Wight was late nineteenth-century Britain's answer to the Hamptons and much in vogue, since Queen Victoria and her family would regularly decamp to Osborne House, their home on the island. This connection, albeit rather tenuous, was enough to ensure that my poetic education was almost entirely Tennysonian. However, this did not involve a critical acquaintance with the work; rather, I remember happy afternoons spent illustrating and illuminating "The Lady of Shalott" and "The Eagle," which we had laboriously copied out longhand in order to practice writing with our leaky ink pens. My young fingers were perpetually stained royal blue.

My first forays into the active study of literature a few years later were far from illustrious. While moving a few years ago I discovered my school reports from the ages of six to sixteen, and the English Literature entries include such comments as, "She has a cavalier disregard for accuracy and form," "Her spelling is bizarre [and] her experience of language is narrow," and, my favorite, "she wastes too much time organizing the whereabouts of her books and general classroom impedimenta." I still procrastinate by organizing my impedimenta. Any literature studied up to that age had been entirely British (Shakespeare for the most part) and largely historically remote. The most recent verse allowed to enter my purview was the (entirely British) poetry of the First World War.

My first encounter with both contemporary and American poetry came in 1992 at St Albans School. Founded in 948, the school is one of the oldest in world, boasts such alumni as Stephen Hawking and Nicholas Breakspear (latterly know as Pope Adrian IV), and at the time was know for its rather maverick and free-wheeling approach to educational standards (that era is now, sadly, long past). The school, overthrowing more than a thousand years of tradition, had just started to let girls attend the school; there were sixteen of us new girls and eight hundred boys. It was housed in a series of gorgeous buildings made out of the blue-grey flint found in the nearby Chiltern Hills, the oldest of which was the castle-like Abbey Gateway. The medieval Gateway had arrowslits and holes through which to poor boiling oil on one's enemies. These architectural features must have come in handy during the Peasants' Revolt of 1381, when disgruntled lower orders stormed the

Abbey. I adored it there. Most of all I adored my English teacher, John Mole, who was the first actual real-life poet I'd ever met. On the first day of class he distributed copies of George MacBeth's Longman anthology *Poetry 1900–1975*. A complete revelation: apparently poetry also existed in America and was being written up to as recently as the year before my birth! So taken was I with the book that I pilfered the school's copy and still have it in my office in Houston. It that class that I was to read the poem that set me on the path to becoming a poetry critic: W. H. Auden's "In Memory of W. B. Yeats" (1939).

My relationship with Auden's poem has developed over the past twenty-five years and my academic career has, in many ways, been defined by the various insights and illuminations won from a near-daily interaction with his great elegy for Yeats. It provided me with the central arguments relating to prosody and elegy that I explore in my book *Grief and Meter* and furnishes me with the title of this book, which comes from these lines from the very middle of the poem:

> For poetry makes nothing happen: it survives
> In the valley of its making where executives
> Would never want to tamper, flows on south
> From ranches of isolation and the busy griefs,
> Raw towns that we believe and die in; it survives,
> A way of happening, a mouth.

It is in these lines that Auden sets the agenda for poetry after 1939, heralding a new age for poetry in which the poem is not a product, a well-wrought urn to be admired as an aesthetic object but rather a participatory process, a "flow" a "way of happening." Moreover, not just an act rather than a object, but also an act that "makes nothing happen."

I've considered Auden's assertion at length in my earlier work, so I don't want to rehash that here (you can find some discussion of it in chapter I); suffice it to say that I've been grappling with it for the best part of three decades now, but it wasn't until very recently that I noticed, upon untangling the syntax of this passage for the hundredth time, that though poetry "survives" in the "valley of its making" (a phrase that has received plenty of critical debate since Auden was to change it to "making" from "saying" in later incarnations of the poem) poetry comes directly "from ranches of isolation and the busy griefs." And then, recognizing with shock that I'd spent most of my professional life trying to reconcile those "busy griefs" with the elegiac poems born of them that I reflected anew on that familiar line and I was struck by the strangeness of the word "ranches."

Ranches. Ranch. To my English ears it is the most ineffably American word I can imagine. It comes from the American Spanish "rancho," meaning farmhouse. Yet the Americanized version of the word is freighted with so much more than that. From its humble roots in the nineteenth century (according to the *Oxford English Dictionary*, in a letter of 28 August 1846 one B. Upton writes, "Rancheros are farmers and a farm house is called a ranch") the word takes on a new life in the twentieth century thanks to marketers keen to capitalize on the word's associations with American resourcefulness and frontier spirit. In the fifties the cookie-cutter open-plan bungalows of the American suburbs become "ranch style" homes. In the nineties and onward in America, one of the most ubiquitous condiments one can dip one's victuals in is Ranch dressing (which, I would like to inform our American viewers, is all but unknown to the rest of civilization, and rightly so, because it is an abomination). But what did that particularly American word "ranch" mean to Auden in January 1939, eight months before he sat in a "dive" (also a uniquely American locus) on "Fifty-second street / Uncertain and afraid"?

Certainly in 1939 "ranch" was as distinctively an American word as another word used in the poem, "Bourse" (the Paris stock exchange), was French. It clearly had, in Auden's mind, those very associations with independence, and, of course, isolation that those canny ad men would later co-opt for their own purposes. In the poem it functions as a symbol of the frontier of Auden's imagination in 1939, newly arrived in America after leaving the Europe of the "public statutes" and "fashionable quays" of the poem behind. Thus the poem's geographical references enact the transatlantic voyage that the poet himself has just taken. Most significantly it is from this American frontier that poetry is flowing; a current that has, indeed, proved to be the prevailing influence in twentieth-century verse.

There have been few studies of Anglo-American poetic relations. As the British poet and editor Jeff Nutall asserted, "the academic capsule was almost perfectly sealed"; the intellectual compartmentalizations of our traditions approaching near-quarantine conditions. In their introduction to the essay collection *Something We Have That They Don't: British and American Poetic Relations* (2004) the editors Steve Clark and Mark Ford consider why this might be:

> The paucity of studies addressing literary interrelations ... is indicative of an apparent reluctance to analyze in detail the traffic in poetic rhetoric between the two countries. Both British and American critics seem more comfortable with narratives that define their respective poetries in isolation from each other, and this separation has come to be institutionalized in universities on both sides of the Atlantic.

Once again, that idea of "isolation" that Auden attaches to the idea of American ranches in his poem. That the jet stream of poetic power has been prevailingly from west to east across the ocean is undeniable and has been considered in work such as Keith Tuma's *Fishing by Obstinate Isles* (1998) in which he considers the lack of influence of British poetry on its American readership. Certainly, in my experience as a Limey professor of contemporary poetry at Stateside universities, in large part the recent poetry of the British Isles is very rarely taught, and this is an omission that I seek to correct at every available opportunity.

In many ways I had regretfully accepted that critically entrenched isolationist version of events, considering myself an anomaly, a salmon who had swum against the current upstream from the small pond of British verse into the great lake of American poetry (easier for a poetry critic than an actual poet, perhaps?). Indeed, I was propelled across the Atlantic by American rather than English poetry. It was, after all, the Robert Lowell archive held at the Houghton Library at Harvard University that ultimately led to me being a Visiting Fellow there and leaving behind my beloved London.

When the editor of this series, the venerable Robert Archambeau, approached me with the idea of collecting together some of the articles and as-yet-unpublished scribblings of my past two decades I was delighted but also concerned. Would my critical miscellany be rejected like the pudding that Winston Churchill sent back for lacking a theme? It was with great surprise, then, that upon mining the dusty hard drives of long-abandoned laptops an abiding theme emerged that I then expanded on in a series of new essays about things I'd wanted to write about for ages, such as the fate of the Irish poet in America; the significance of the T. S. Eliot Prize for Poetry and the differing role of the poet laureate in the U.S. and the UK. It turns out that, over the course of my career in the writings collected and greatly expanded here for the first time, I have been concocting, for the most part entirely unwittingly, a veritable transatlantic trifle.

I have been continually drawn to consider transatlantic poetics and the dynamics of influence at play between Britain, Ireland and America. I am fascinated by those poets—such as W. H. Auden, Robert Lowell, Joseph Brodsky, and Thom Gunn—whose careers have bridged the Atlantic and who shared my own expatriated state. That expatriated condition, in my case, is complicated by my Anglo-Irish identity and I frequently find myself compelled to write about the work of those, such as Seamus Heaney and Paul Muldoon, who share it. Even when firmly on American soil I seem always to hover near the boundaries and borders; considering, for example, Susan Howe's exploration of the legacy of British colonialism in the Adirondacks in *Thorow* or asking why foreign poets such as Wisława Szymborska frequently seem much better able to write about the events of 9/11 than American ones.

In the first of this book's five sections I will revisit "the obstinate isles" that Pound wrote of in "Hugh Selwyn Mauberley." Tuma, of course, used the phrase as the title of a book that considered why American readers were relegating British poetry to (unwarranted) irrelevance. Eighteen years later I'd like to enforce his corrective by revisiting our obstinate poetics and poetry. I then turn, in the book's second part to consider the transatlantic remit of the T. S. Eliot Prize for Poetry and then, in the third section the idea of "Transatlantic Traffic" by considering two major acts of poetic expatriation across the Atlantic: Thom Gunn's move to America in his youth and Ezra Pound's exile to Italy in old age. "*Au Contraire,*" the fourth portion of this collection, considers the vexed and frequently misunderstood nature of the Anglo-Irish, or rather, as I have it, the Irish-English poet. Finally, in "So Large, So Friendly and So Rich" I provide an outsider's take on the U. S. poetry scene. I hope that despite the isolationist claims of poets and critics on both sides of the Atlantic this book will delineate how our respective recent poetic traditions are highly interdependent and demonstrate why that is a desirable state of affairs.

I.
The Obstinate Isles Revisited

Explainers, Idiots and Laureates

On the death of Sir John Betjeman in 1984 the Poet Laureateship of Britain was offered to Philip Larkin, who turned it down. He was in good company: since its inception in 1668 Thomas Gray, William Mason, Samuel Rogers, William Morris and Sir Walter Scott have also refused the honor. William Wordsworth accepted the role on the condition he didn't have to write anything to order; which is exactly what he did. On learning that Ted Hughes had accepted the position Larkin sniffed, "I like Ted, but in a just society he wouldn't be the Poet Laureate, he'd be the village idiot." Other than delighting in Larkin's bitchiness, both his barb and his refusal also reveal much about the role of Laureate. Larkin's comment and the idea of the poetic "village" also calls to mind another delicious literary slight; Gertrude Stein's dismissive comment about Ezra Pound: "A village explainer, excellent if you were a village, but if you were not, not." Of course, there was absolutely no chance of Pound ever being appointed in any official capacity by the American government after his trial for treason, but in many ways his "village explainer" impulses are exactly what the role demands.

The Laureateship is a poisoned and prized chalice, a thankless and often reviled task and yet also a great honor. It is an antiquated and feudal position that requires the holder of the office to respond to contemporary, and, in the UK, royal and military events. It is the very embodiment of the much-slighted genre of "occasional verse," and, as Thom Gunn points out in his essay on Ben Jonson, isn't all poetry, to some degree, occasional? And how can any poet be expected to reliably rise to the occasion? Not that the incumbents don't realize the awfulness of their illustrious predicament; Sir John Betjeman attempted an invocation in a letter to cure his writers' block-stricken brain, "Oh God, the Royal poem!! Send the H[oly] G[host] to help me over that fence. So far no sign: Watch and pray." Ted Hughes agonized over the Faustian bargain for a number of days before agreeing to assume the position, "my first pure thought was 'Here we go—how horrible.' Just dismay ... I really felt I'd walked into a pit trap. I saw at once that refusing invoked as many demons as accepting." Some, like Andrew Motion, approach the job somewhat more blithely in the face of governmental and monarchical assurances, "The first time I met the Queen she said the same thing as Tony Blair, whom I'd also just met for the first time: 'You don't have to do anything.'" One rather wishes he'd listened to their advice.

Certainly, the laureateship has been responsible for creating some cracking British verse such as Tennyson's "Charge of the Light Brigade" and his "Ode on the Death of the Duke of Wellington." Yet for every beloved classic there are ten clunkers including some truly ghastly stuff. After Tennyson's death the office remained fallow for a period of four years as a mark of respect before a virtually unknown poet, Alfred Austin, took on the task. Austin was considered to be a political appointee, rewarded for his support of the Conservative Prime Minister, Lord Salisbury. Certainly his poetry didn't merit it; some of it, like "Jameson's Ride" (about an early British skirmish against the Boer in South Africa, the very same incident that inspired Rudyard Kipling's "If") approaches William McGonagall-esque clunkiness: "I suppose we were wrong, were madmen, / Still I think at the Judgment Day, / When God sifts the good from the bad men, / There'll be something more to say." He is now best known, poor chap, due to the erroneous attribution to him of this couplet on the illness of the Prince of Wales: "Across the wires the electric message came: / 'He is no better. He is much the same.'" Apocryphal it may be; but fitting, so it stuck. Betjeman's "Inland Waterway," on the glorious occasion of the Queen Mother reopening a canal, concludes with these deathly lines, "Your Majesty, our friend for many years, / Confirms a triumph now the moment nears: / The lock you have reopened will set free / The heart of England to the open sea." Of particular noteworthiness in the category of recent appalling Laureate verse one need look no further than Motion's cringe-inducing and rap-inspired "On the Record" on Prince William's 21st birthday: "Better stand back / Here's an age attack, / But the second in line / Is dealing with it fine."

There's also inevitably an issue of audience; an audience that both clamors for a fitting tribute and yet cannot but be critical of it. As

Ted Hughes grumbled in a letter a few years after his appointment, "I understand the dislike. Verse written semi-privately or as if semi-privately to someone else and yet published openly is always somehow offensive.... Who can write in an amiable way to any member of the royal family without it looking like flattery? Can't be done." Since the British monarch is also the head of State and appoints one to the role (after consulting with the Prime Minister), it is also to some degree, a politicized role and therefore inevitably controversial. This, after all, is why the Catholic convert John Dryden was sacked in 1688 when the Protestant William and Mary ascended to the throne. Seamus Heaney, though born one of her Majesty's subjects, definitively put himself out of the running by becoming an Irish citizen (though Irish poets, such as Nahum Tate, could be appointed to the role when the South was still part of the UK prior to the creation of the Irish Republic). In his letters Ted Hughes comments, "I'm very aware, too, of its (ghostly) political dimensions.... Philip L. might have seemed like too obvious an unfurling of the banner over the far right." The current incumbent since 2009, Dame Carol Ann Duffy, was considered during the previous round of deliberations after Hughes's death in 1998. She is the first woman to hold the role in the UK (the first female Laureate in the U.S. was Maxine Kumin in 1981). Duffy was not appointed sooner, however, apparently due to Tony Blair's reservations that she was too Scottish and gay for middle England and, one assumes, the "New" Labour electorate. Beyond the obviously Royalist tenor of the gig there's also an inescapable aspect of English-centric Nationalism. The royally appointed laureate is that of the United Kingdom of Great Britain and Northern Ireland but the nations under that unifying (for now) banner have their own parallel official roles with competitive and performative customs. The tradition of the Scots Makar runs back to the fifteenth century; the Welsh Bardds would fight it out at the National Eisteddfod; while the Irish Saoi were responsible not only for writing poetry but also for reciting and conveying the canon.

So why take on the job? Certainly, in Britain at least, not for the money. In the UK, Laureates are traditionally appointed for an unlimited term and a fixed sum: a modest annual payment and a

Falstaffian "butt of Sack" (this amounts to several hundred bottles of sherry). In one of Kingsley Amis's irreverent and scatological missives to Larkin, Kingsley ribs him, "take it you've come round about the L'ship now they're talking about a £10thou tax-free stipend, you greedy old bumrag." Turns out though even a raise in the honorarium wasn't enough to get Larkin to take on the gig. At least in recent years it's not an "until-death-do-us-part" affair (the longest-serving Laureate, Tennyson, was *in situ* for forty-two years), now the term has been limited to ten years on the recommendation of Paul Muldoon in his capacity as head of the UK Poetry Society. This seems fairer on the incumbent, and, mercifully, their readership.

The process of the appointment of the laureate invariably provokes a ferment of newspaper opinion pieces about those in the running and the position in general. One of the very best insights into Laureateship, however, is not an op-ed, but rather Tony Harrison's scathing take-down poem "Laureate's Block (for Queen Elizabeth)." The avowedly Republican Harrison had, extraordinarily, been in the running for the Laureateship after the death of Hughes in October 1998 and the poem is a definitive rejection not only of the job but of the monarchy too. "There should be no successor to Ted Hughes" writes Harrison, "Nor should Prince Charles succeed our present queen / and spare us some toad's ode on coronation. / I'd like all suchlike odes there've ever been, / binned by a truly democratic nation." The block of the title, therefore, is not only the one writerly one that gripped Betjeman and Motion when confronted with the demands of the position but also that of the Republican executioner's:

> (I'd hoped last week that would-be royal hacks
> that self-promoting sycophantic flock
> would whet their talents on the headsman's axe
> but it seems like a bad case of laureate's block—
> 30th January 1649
> though it's hard to use the date for self-promotion
> the anniversary's gone by with not a line
> from toadies like Di-deifying Motion.)

The date, of course, is that of the execution of the first King Charles. Harrison damningly identifies toadying and self-promotion as the motivation behind poets like, "Di-deifying Motion." Motion, perhaps auditioning for the role, had already written "Mythology" on the death of Princess Diana in 1997. Instead of any of his contemporaries Harrison looks to an earlier poet as an exemplar, Thomas Gray, who refused the Laureateship in 1757 after the death of Colley Cibber (a poet best know to posterity for the savage satirization he received from Alexander Pope's pen in *The Dunciad*) and Harrison quotes at length from a letter of Gray's from 19 December 1757 in "Laureate's Block":

> Though I very well know the bland emollient saponaceous qualities of sack and silver, yet if any great man would say to me 'I make you rat-catcher to his Majesty, with a salary of £300 a year and two butts of the best Malaga; and though it has been usual to catch a mouse or two, for form's sake, in public once a year, yet to you, sir, we shall not stand upon these things' I cannot say I should jump at it, nay, if they would drop the very name of the office, and call me Sinecure to the King's Majesty, I should still feel a little awkward, and think everybody I saw smelt a rat about me.... The office itself has always humbled the professor hitherto (even in an age when kings were somebody), if he were a poor writer by making him more conspicuous, and if he were a good one by setting him at war with the little fry of his own profession, for there are poets little enough to envy even a poet laureat.

Harrison's withering poetic rejection of the role and Gray's epistolary reservations pinpoint exactly the problem at stake with the British laureateship: its seemingly inextricable association with the monarchy, problematic even centuries ago when Royalty were regarded as infallible, untenable in the modern, much diminished, era of monarchy heralded by the abdication crisis and followed up by a shocking series of personal revelations and all-too-human failings on the part of the royal family. Perhaps we should've heeded Edward Gibbon in his note in *The Decline and Fall of the Roman Empire* on the coronation of Petrarch at the Capitol in Rome in 1341 CE: "I much doubt whether any age or court can produce a similar establishment of a stipendiary poet, who in every reign, and at all events, is bound to furnish twice a year a measure of praise and verse.... the best time for abolishing this ridiculous custom is while the prince is a man of virtue and the poet a man of genius."

I am not arguing, as Gibbon is, for the abolition of the role but rather for the role to be remodeled and revivified in the UK; how best to do this? Well, let's look at a case study of what happens when the role is divorced from royalty right here on our doorstep in the case of the American Laureateship. That role was established as "The Consultant in Poetry to the Library of Congress" in 1936 and the title was changed to "Poetry Laureate Consultant in Poetry to the Library of Congress" in 1985. The position is usually for a year (though there are several exceptions such as Robert Pinsky who serve over a few consecutive years) and the annual honorarium is currently $35,000. There is no alcoholic stipend whatsoever. Unlike the UK also, the appointed poet is not expected to produce occasional poems of celebration, but rather the Library of Congress takes care to "afford each incumbent maximum freedom to work on his or her own projects while at the Library." Usually the laureate engages in a series of readings at the Library of Congress and works as an Ambassador for the cause of poetry in America. Some have written about national events—such as Billy Collins' "The Names" about the events of September 11th, 2001—but it is by no means expected or required.

This is all very well and clearly preferable to the mess we're in over the pond but that is not to say that the role has been entirely uncontroversial. Though divorced from the Executive branch that has not entirely insulated the Laureate from political problems. Of particular note is the furor around William Carlos Williams' appointment in 1952. Williams was suffering from poor health after a heart attack in 1948 when he accepted the role, but he was never allowed to assume it due to the McCarthy witch-hunts. Williams was found to have engaged in pro-Russian "anti-American" activities (in his case signing a petition in support of Russia back when that nation was still an ally of the United States) and therefore his tenure was blocked. The Laureateship would remain unfilled until the end of the McCarthy reign of intellectual terror in 1956.

The most frequently leveled recent criticism of the role comes, however, not from politicians but rather from poets, those "unacknowledged legislators of the world" who, in the case of the Laureateship, would, it appears, like to legislate for increased inclusivity and against what is perceived to be the poetic "establishment." This mistrust about the officalization of verse in America reached its zenith in 2001 after the appointment of Billy Collins to the role. Collins, though a widely read and wildly successful poet, is not universally admired by his peers; his crowd-pleasing poetry is often held up as an example of the "bland emollient saponaceous qualities" of silver if not sack. His populist appointment led to great debate on the SUNY Buffalo poetics listserv (at the time this was akin to an electronic version of the Forum of Rome) where the anointing of an anti-establishment "anti-laureate" was mooted. This debate was also paralleled in the UK at around the same time after the appointment of Motion. The Brits plumped for the nomenclature of a "shadow-Laureate" which, I think, has pleasingly and fittingly sinister resonances.

Meanwhile, back at the ranch, Robert Archambeau (the High Commissioner of the United States Anti-Laureate Commission) laid out the rules: "All poets are eligible (non-US poets too), except those with Iowa MFAs, Pulitzer Prizes, or strong personal ties to Helen Vendler." The prize, pleasingly reinstating the British alcoholic beverage tithe, was to be one bottle of vodka. Great debate ensued, in particular regarding the "Iowa Exclusion," since, as Barrett Watten convincingly argued, "A poet might get a very focused view of precisely the system of representation that makes laureatehood politically dubious precisely at the Iowa Workshop." The very idea of being "anti" also took some flack: surely what was being proposed was "alternative" rather than truly anti? Ultimately, "with all the ironies and contradictions appertaining there unto," Anselm Hollo was announced to be the anointed one and was to be the first and last anti-laureate of America.

So what is to be done? Comparing and contrasting the transatlantic state of laureateship and taking into account the anti-laureate debate, several pertinent issues—and possible solutions to those problems—arise. Of course, the compromise I propose for both the British and American Laureateships is by no means perfect, but I do hope that it will start a productive debate.

Undoubtedly Gray is right when he asserts, "The office itself has always humbled the professor hitherto (even in an age when kings were somebody)." The position is always going to be almost impossible no matter how many tweaks might be made, but one of the most important changes I would suggest is that the position of Laureate must be beyond the reach of patronage, be it monarchical or presidential. The problem has been that the occasional and personal nature of the verse that the onslaught of Royal events in the UK requires has muddied the importance of, and need for, public occasional verse. The American Laureateship's insulation from the Executive wing and the influence of the President is particularly helpful in this instance, but there is also a further consideration and intriguing exception: that of the inaugural poem.

Inaugural poems are a very particular subgenre of occasional poems. Their history start with a serendipitous failure: the elderly Robert Frost's inability to read the poem he had composed for the occasion of President Kennedy's inauguration in 1961 in the glaring light of a sunny snow-bound January morning. Instead of being able to read his new poem composed for the occasion, "A Dedication," he recited "The Gift Outright" from memory. Frost's poem is intensely problematic with its assertion that, "The land was ours before we were the land's," and its espousal of manifest destiny. Yet, as controversial as its claims are, it is significant in setting the historical and nationalizing tenor of those inaugural poems that have followed it. Since Frost four further poets have composed such poems; all have been for Democratic presidents-elect: Maya Angelou's "On the Pulse of the Morning" for Clinton; Miller Williams's "Of History and Hope" for Clinton's second inauguration; "Praise Song for the Day" by Elizabeth Alexander for Obama's first inauguration and Richard Blanco's "One

Today" for his second. None of these of these poems address the president in any way, but rather the state of the nation as a whole. This is central to all of these much-discussed poems; it is shared by those widely regarded to be successful attempts (such as the Angelou poem, with its encompassing of the nation's pre-Anthropocene and native American history) and those generally regarded to be unsuccessful (such as Franco's, with its excessively personal focus on his own family's experience and, as many argued, the tasteless inclusion of the Sandy Hook massacre). The popularity of and interest in the inaugural poem reveals that people very much want public occasional verse, but these poems should address the nation and the lives of the people rather than the life of a figurehead. So I propose that the role should come with a requirement for a certain amount of occasional poems on national events but not political events.

I think the Americans are correct in giving the Laureate a living and honest wage. To do so underscores the significance and importance of the role. As charmed as I am by the butt of sack and the bottle of vodka, I'm afraid any vestige of atavistic or feudal trappings opens the position to ridicule and accusations of irrelevance. The matter of term as well as remuneration is also key. With a mere one year in the U.S. and a whole ten years in the UK we are far from the Goldilocks zone of productive and sustainable conditions. I would suggest that a term of three years, renewable for one time to a total of six, should be knocking it out of the park in Tennysonian fashion.

The thing I would like to most vociferously underscore in this reimagining of the position of the Poet Laureate is the importance of the role itself. Many of the attacks on the Laureateship in the UK (such as those of Gay and Harrison) come from those who take issue with the Royalist nature of the role. The suggestions outlined above would obviate those objections. Other reservations about the Laureateship tend to come from within and from other poets and critics. I think at particular issue is what Gray identified on rejecting the post: even were one to be good at the job it would set him or her "at war with the little fry of his own profession, for there are poets little enough to envy even a poet laureat." However, if the honest wage for this impossible job comes from the legislative wing—Congress, as it already does in the U.S., or the House of Commons in the UK rather than the purse of the monarch—the poet should be answerable first and foremost to the people and not their peers or patrons. This is something that Hughes intimates in this thoughtful letter to Jack Brown on his predicament in 1987:

> It interests me to hear how other people regard the Laureateship business. I'm impressed, very much, by the way almost everybody take it seriously. It's extremely peculiar that people who have no interest in poetry nevertheless have strong instinctive feelings about this.

Those strong instinctive feelings and need for a "village explainer" are clearly apparent in people's reactions to the inaugural poem and our societies need someone appointed to speak to and for them. Not only that, but I'd also argue that anything that foregrounds and underscores the significance of poetry and by extension the humane (NB, Republican presidents-elect) can only be a boon to society. I'd like to end by giving the final word on the subject to Kingsley Amis, in another letter to Philip Larkin. In it, he tells Larkin of how people keep coming up to him into the Garrick (a members' club in London where he would often lunch) saying, "This chap Hughes, he isn't half no good is he? Y'know, talking of the old po[etry]: in gen[eral]." Even if Larkin does think Hughes a village idiot, as silly and saponaceous as the idea of Laureate may be, anything that gets people to talk "of the old po: in gen" is enormously useful.

"Breaking Bread with the Dead":
W. H. Auden, Seamus Heaney, and Yeats's Legacy

In his commonplace book *A Certain World* (1970), W. H. Auden observed that, "Poets seem to be more generally successful at writing elegies than any other literary genre. Indeed, the only elegy I know of which seems to me a failure is 'Adonais.'" This "failure" is elucidated in an earlier essay, "Yeats as an Example" (1948), in which Auden identifies and explores W. B. Yeats's poetic legacy. He argues that Yeats's greatest achievement was to transmute the "occasional poem" from "an official performance of impersonal virtuosity or a trivial *vers de société*" into "a serious reflective poem of at once personal and public interest." To illustrate his point he compared Yeats's elegy "In Memory of Major Robert Gregory" (1918) with Shelley's "Adonais" (1821). The former, he argues, "never loses the personal note of a man speaking about his personal friends in a particular setting [...] and at the same time the occasion and the characters acquire a symbolic public significance," whereas he finds that in "Adonais," "both Shelley and Keats disappear as people." Thus, Auden deems "Adonais" to have failed in its poetic purpose not only because the dead poet disappears twice, first in death itself and then again behind the elegy's devices and didacticism, but also because the living poet is subsumed by his own act of commemoration. Though Auden saw Yeats's greatest poetic achievement as the resistance to the disappearance of the elegized and the elegist, in the first line of "In Memory of W. B. Yeats" (1939), we read not of the poet's death, but of how he "disappeared in the dead of winter." Before a close reading of the opposing influences of disappearance and survival in Auden's elegy and the influence of Shelley's "Adonais" upon it, we will look briefly at Yeats's elegiac legacy.

In his landmark study of the genre, *The English Elegy* (1985), Peter Sacks pinpoints "In Memory of Major Robert Gregory" (1918) as the early twentieth-century elegy that "dispensed with many of the comforting fictions of the genre." Yeats plays with our elegiac expectations by adhering in many aspects to generic convention, yet ultimately rejects the consolatory function such conventions had, traditionally, served. In the twelfth and final stanza the poem ruptures and Yeats's grief can no longer be formalized, causing the poem to be truncated like the life that it ostensibly celebrates:

> I had thought, seeing how bitter is that wind
> That shakes the shutter, to have brought to mind
> All those that manhood tried, or childhood loved
> Or boyish intellect approved,
> With some appropriate commentary on each;
> Until imagination brought
> A fitter welcome; but a thought
> Of that late death took all my heart for speech.

No longer does grief set the elegiac process into motion, but rather vice versa. The poet must rely upon —"I had thought"—the elegiac conceit of the pathetically fallacious "bitter wind" rattling the shutter to prompt remembrance and bring to mind episodes to recall in the proper elegiac fashion with "some appropriate commentary on each," so as to fulfill generic expectations. Yet Yeats does not need the elegiac element to recall and recreate Gregory. The young man is still very much in his mind and "but a thought" of his death silences the poet, while yet, at the same time, prompting Yeats to a consummate act of speech. The dead now seem all too close and cannot be constrained by the depersonalizing conventions of consolation.

Yet perhaps it is another of Yeats's poems that has had a far more profound elegiac influence his successors: "Under Ben Bulben" (1938). Though not an elegy occasioned by the death another, Yeats's late poem functions like a preemptive elegy, which not only attempts to control his posthumous influence on, and reception from, future generations, but also dictates to inheritors from beyond the grave, instructing:

> Irish poets, learn your trade,
> Sing whatever is well made,

> Scorn the sort now growing up
> All out of shape from toe to top,
> Their unremembering hearts and heads
> Base-born products of base beds.

Yeats seals his self-designed sepulcher by inscribing what would go on to be his own epitaph: *"Cast a cold eye / On life, on death. / Horseman, pass by!"* Yeats's contingent and ambivalent elegy for Gregory, along with his self-elegy "Under Ben Bulben," created the elegiac agenda that Auden was to address in his poem for the dead poet.

"Yeats as an Example" and "In Memory of W. B. Yeats"

In "Yeats as an Example" Auden is acutely concerned with the dynamics of artistic inheritance and the reaction of the poet to the work of other poets, living and dead. Auden uses Yeats as an example rather than as an exemplar, and though he takes care to pinpoint his poetic legacy as the synthesis of the personal and symbolic within elegy, this appraisal is undermined by an assertion that prefaces it: "When a poet [...] reads a poem written by another, he is apt to be less concerned with what the latter actually accomplished by his poem than with the suggestions it throws out upon how he, the reader, may solve the poetic problems which confront him now." The "poetic problems" that the figure of Yeats had posed Auden as an elegist nine years previously were twofold: Yeats had already attempted to enshrine his reputation in an elegy of his own fashioning, and the politics that he had espoused were deeply problematic for anyone that sought to address his legacy. In later years Auden could joke in the final stanza of "Academic Graffiti" (1952):

> To get the Last Poems of Yeats,
> You need not mug up on dates;
> All a reader requires
> Is some knowledge of gyres
> And the sort of people he hates.

However, in 1939, the year of Yeats's death and the eve of the Second World War, his political views threatened to damage irreparably his reputation as a poet. It was through his elegy that Auden would attempt to answer these problems, and reassert Yeats's poetic potency, in the very form that Yeats modified for the twentieth century and made available to his successors: that of the personal and yet symbolically significant elegy.

Auden argues in "Yeats as an Example" that "former hero-worship, as in other spheres of life, is all too apt to turn into an equally excessive hostility and contempt" and goes on to diagnose the problem inherent in such antipathy: "As long as we harbor such a resentment, it will be a dangerous hindrance to our own poetic development, for, in poetry as in life, to lead one's own life means to relive the lives of one's parents and, through them, of all one's ancestors; the duty of the present is neither to copy nor to deny the past but to resurrect it."

"In Memory of W. B. Yeats" demonstrates how an elegy for another poet can fulfill a cathartic function, by rehabilitating the reputation of the dead poet also by helping the living exorcise any resentment that they may feel toward their immediate precursors (there are very few anxious elegies addressed to the shades of long-dead poets). In this way an elegy for a precursor poet, which on first reading may appear agonistic, could ultimately be restorative rather than reactionary. The dialectic that Auden established in his criticism between copying and denying is particularly informative and, as we shall see, Auden resurrects and rehabilitates the image of Yeats in his elegy by alternating between these two impulses.

Auden concludes his argument in "Yeats as an Example" by comparing Yeats to Gerard Manley Hopkins. He finds Hopkins to be a "minor poet," arguing that his innovations in form were so idiosyncratic as to be an aesthetic dead end, and therefore concludes, "he cannot influence later poets in any fruitful way; they can only imitate him." However, he contends that Yeats is, though problematic, a "major poet," since he "not only attempts to solve new problems, but the problems he attacks are central to the tradition, and the lines along which he attacks them, while they are his own, are not idiosyncratic, but produce results which are available to his successors." We will now explore how Auden engages with the "results" that Yeats's legacy made available to him, and how he attacks the problem not only of reconciling Yeats the man to his poems, but also the larger problem, "central to the tradition," of how to elegize a precursor. We will then address Auden's allusions to his other elegiac forebears, with particular reference to Shelley's elegiac approach to Keats, and finally examine the manner in which the "results" that Auden attained in "In Memory of W. B. Yeats" were to make Yeats's poetic legacy approachable and available to Seamus Heaney.

W. H. Auden sailed into New York Harbor on 26 January 1939. Two days later, W. B. Yeats died in Roquebrune on the French Riviera and was buried far from his preordained spot under the shadow of Ben Bulben in County Sligo. Though composed on 4 September 1938, "Under Ben Bulben" was first published in *The Irish Times* on 3 February 1939. "In Memory of W. B. Yeats" initially appeared in *The New Republic* on 8 March 1939. This version omits the second of the poem's three sections (the stanza which starts "You were silly like us.") Auden submitted the manuscript of "The Public v. the Late Mr. W. B. Yeats," a critical appraisal of the dead poet's greatness, to *The Partisan Review* on 18 March 1939. In *Later Auden* Edward Mendelson plausibly speculates that the second section of "In Memory of W. B. Yeats" was composed at roughly the same time. The poem was published in its final tripartite form (though not its final version, discussed below, which was published in 1966 in Auden's *Collected Shorter Poems 1927–1957*) in *The London Mercury* in April 1939.

"In Memory of W. B. Yeats" was to be an inaugural and catalytic poem for Auden. It was the first poem that he wrote on the cusp of his new life in America, and it was to initiate an elegiac frenzy that would last for a year, during which time he would go on to write poems for Voltaire (February 1939), Herman Melville (March 1939), the playwright Ernst Toller (May 1939), and Sigmund Freud (September 1939). "In Memory of W. B. Yeats" draws much of its potency from earlier elegies for poets, in particular the very elegy that Auden appears to discountenance in an act of classic Bloomian misprision: "Adonais." However, before Auden was able to show how, "The words of a dead man / Are modified in the guts of the living," he had to disinter the dead poet from a poetic tomb of his own creation: "Under Ben Bulben." Ironically, it was to be through the assimilation of Yeats's innovation of personal individuation in elegy that Auden was to exhume the figure of the dead poet from his self-ordained place in the canon. Thus, Auden's elegy performs an act of restoration on, rather than desecration of, the reputation that Yeats had attempted to place beyond the reach of his successors.

In *The Life of the Poet: Beginning and Ending Poetic Careers*, Lawrence Lipking contends that the first section of "In Memory of W. B. Yeats" is notable in the "utterly un-Yeatsian way in which it commemorates Yeats," as it denies the style, form and tone of Yeats's poetics. Auden describes a frost-bound landscape, like that of "Adonais," but instead of a pastoral locus, Yeats's death takes place in a frozen urban wasteland far from the mystical settings of his poems. Auden immediately set Yeats not in the context of death, as "Adonais" does with Keats in its first line ("I weep for Adonais—he is dead!"), but rather in the far more modern contexts of loss and absence: "He disappeared in the dead of winter." Indeed, the first death that we read of in the poem is not that of the poet but rather that of the "dying day." In the first stanza of "Adonais" time also dies, as the hour of Keats's death is commanded by Shelley to tell of how, "with me / Died Adonais." In "Adonais" we read that "Grief made the young Spring wild, and she threw down / Her kindling buds, as if she Autumn were." In Auden's elegy the pathetic fallacy is updated, and mechanical "instruments" are anthropomorphized and able to "agree / The day of his death was a dark cold day." Nature seems indifferent to the poet's death, as "Far from his illness / The wolves ran on through the evergreen forests." Unlike the deciduous trees of Shelley's spring, Auden's evergreen woods will never shed their buds in imitation of autumn. Mendelson suggests that the wolves hark back to "the grim wolf with privy paw" in Milton's "Lycidas." However, Auden's pack of wolves may owe far more to Shelley's metaphorical transformation of Keats's critics in "Adonais" into "herded wolves, bold only to pursue," since Auden follows this line with a passage concerned with the ways in which Yeats's work will be read and received after his death.

As Auden begins to set the scene not only of the poet's death, but also of the ongoing life of his work, he repeatedly refers to elegiac convention through the very act of subverting generic expectations and motifs. In this way he modifies the words of not only Yeats, but also of other dead poets, and particularly those of Shelley, in his own guts. The ancient elegiac conceit of pastoral artificiality had caused Shelley and Keats to disappear in "Adonais," and though "In Memory of W. B. Yeats" starts with a disappearance, the survival of the poet's words in envisaged in this first section in a landscape both quotidian and contemporaneous. The effect is to normalize rather than distance the death. The autocratic figure of Yeats is brought closer to us in a world we recognize as our own.

Yeats had endeavored to control his posthumous reputation in "Under Ben Bulben" by attempting to create what Lipking has called a "*tombeau*" after Stéphane Mallarmé's exploration of the form. However, as Lipking notes, "Poets may try to design their own memorials, but all they can be sure of is the body of their work; the monument, the way the work will be remembered, must be left to other hands. Very quickly the poet ceases to control his fate." In his final poems Yeats often seems to express fears about losing control over his words. "Under Ben Bulben" lays down the law for Yeats's inheritors, while "The Man and the Echo," is fundamentally concerned with the distortion and misrepresentation of meaning after the moment of utterance. However, this is exactly what Auden celebrates in his elegy. Auden recognizes and—unlike Yeats—accepts that the poet becomes something else in death, and in this acceptance reconfigures notions of literary fame for those that follow him. Death alienates the poet from the body of work which has defined his or her existence. Thus, Yeats's final afternoon of illness is his last one as "himself." On the instant of his death "he became his admirers." His poems only exist "modified" in their "guts" in an act of textual transubstantiation, given over to their interpretations and "unfamiliar affections," beyond authorial intention. Thus, "By mourning tongues /

The death of the poet was kept from his poems" as they continue to exist independently of the life that created them. (However, it must always be remembered that the reader's knowledge of a poet's death inevitably affects his or her reading of their poems.) Jahan Ramazani contends in *The Poetry of Mourning: The Modern Elegy from Hardy to Heaney* that in depicting an artistic rather than otherworldly afterlife Auden "converts Yeats's worry about controlling his inheritance into the key to his immortality," and that as Auden's elegy adopts and adapts Yeats's innovations in the elegiac form it "enacts the theory of reception that [Auden] enunciates." Auden's mourning tongue not only recites, but also ingests Yeats's words, modifying them in his own guts. Thus, as the dead poet becomes his admirers, his admirers, also, to some extent, become him, as they incorporate and resurrect the dead poet's poetics. As Lipking explains, "That equation marks the logic of the *tombeau;* of literary history itself."

Auden takes this most national and mystical of poets and makes him international and demystified. Death encroaches on him like urbanization ("The squares of his mind were empty, / Silence invaded the suburbs") and instead of being interred whole "Under Ben Bulben," he is dismembered and "scattered among a hundred cities" in an act of intellectual atomization. In this Auden appears to owe much to Shelley's description of the nature of literary fame in "Adonais." As Michelle Turner Sharp points out in "Mirroring the Future: Adonais, Elegy, and the Life in Letters.": "Where *Lycidas* posits the false surmise that ushers in a vision of a body lost and broken by the ocean waves, *Adonais* posits the plurality and volatility of reading as what smashes Keats's body into atoms, but also shapes the enduring form of his immortality."

In the earlier stages of inconsolability in "Adonais," the elegizing swain laments that: "The quick Dreams, / The passion-wingéd Ministers of thought, / Who were his flocks [...] Wander no more, from kindling brain to brain." The notion of "kindling" calls to mind the image in Shelley's "Defence of Poetry" of the "mind in creation" as "a fading coal." Shelley posits that it is by the working of "some invisible influence, like an inconstant wind" that awakens the mind to the "transitory brightness" of creation. Keats's ideas are rekindled in the course of "Adonais" not by the "mourning tongues" of his readers, but rather by the "barbed tongues" of his critics, the very tongues that Shelley finds murderous in their critical intent. Auden, unlike Shelley, does not think that criticism kills. Yeats is undone by "illness": both physical, and, as Auden goes on to detail in the latter half of his elegy, intellectual. However, Auden does envisage a critical as well as appreciative reception for the words of the dead man, as his words are, like prisoners of war, "punished under a foreign code of conscience." This reference to criticism not only presages the ideological bent of contemporary critical theory but also subtly turns the tables upon Yeats, who had, in life, subjected Auden to his own critical appraisal.

As editor of *The Oxford Book of Modern Verse: 1892–1935* (1936), Yeats chose to include three of the twenty-nine-year-old Auden's poems in his decidedly idiosyncratic and anachronistic selection: "It's No Use Raising a Shout," "This Lunar Beauty" and "The Silly Fool." However, this was not a gesture of unqualified approval: in his introduction, he suggests that Ezra Pound "has a great influence, more perhaps than any contemporary except Eliot, [and] is probably the source of that lack of form and consequent obscurity which is the main defect of Auden, Day Lewis, and their school." Though he goes on to state that this is "a school which, as will presently be seen, I greatly admire" and cautiously praises Cecil Day Lewis, Charles Madge, Lewis MacNeice, Stephen Spender and George Barker ("I can seldom find more than half a dozen lyrics that I like, yet in this moment of sympathy I prefer them to Eliot"). No further elaboration upon his admiration for Auden is to be found. Might we infer, then, that Yeats thought inclusion in his selection tacit approval enough? Auden does not appear to have shared this opinion. In "The Public v. the Late Mr. William Butler Yeats," Auden's public prosecutor calls *The Oxford Book of Modern Verse* "the most deplorable volume ever issued under the imprint of that highly respected firm."

The idea of the "foreign" is also particularly telling in the context of the self-imposed exile that Auden was writing under.

Yeats's fittingness as an elegiac subject may have been geographical as well as temporal. Not only did the first days of Auden's new life in America overlap with the last days of Yeats's, but in death Yeats also offered Auden an example of the possible fate of the expatriate poet. Mendelson argues that the landscape described in the first few stanzas of "In Memory of W. B. Yeats" is recognizably that of New York harbor, "in the dead of winter, while a light snow disfigured the public statues." However, it could be argued that the topography of the first section owes more to the Old World than the New. The frozen "brooks" of Auden's poem seemed more likely to be tributaries of the Thames than the Hudson, while the "provinces" of Yeats body seems likely to refer to the "Province" of Northern Ireland, and "The squares of his mind" to Dublin's Georgian squares. The Statue of Liberty may be the most widely recognized public statue in the world, but Auden is deliberately unspecific and writes in the plural of how "snow disfigured the public statues." Rather than being a description of New York, Auden's landscape seems to be a direct descendent of James Joyce's depiction of a snow-muffled Dublin in his *Dubliners* short story "The Dead" (1914).

In Joyce's story, Gabriel Conroy points to a statue of Daniel O'Connell, "on which lay patches of snow" on his way home from a family gathering. The allusion not only establishes the theme of Irish insurgence that Auden will go on to develop in the elegy's second section, but also picks up on Joyce's symbolism. In the final paragraph of the "The Dead" the drifting snow elicits an epiphany, as Gabriel Conroy's "soul swooned slowly as he heard the snow falling faintly through the universe and faintly falling, like the descent of their last end, upon all the living and the dead." The "disfiguring" snow of "In Memory of W. B. Yeats" blurs the distinction between the commemorative and the commemorator, the public figure and the private man, and the cityscape of Dublin and New York, as it casts its mantle over the living and the dead. Auden's reference to the French stock exchange, "the Bourse," in this section's final stanza, marks a turn toward the country of Yeats's death, while the "ranches of isolation" and "raw towns" in the poem's second section, seem to take the reader across the Atlantic to the American frontier of Auden's imagination. In the final section of his elegy for Yeats, Auden returns to the "Earth" of Ireland, where the "Irish vessel" of the poet's dead body will rest "emptied of its poetry."

Auden, like Shelley, had not been close in life to the poet he chose to memorialize in death. As Sharp argues, "what concerned Shelley most about Keats was not his fate as a person but as a writer, a fate that Shelley fear he would share." Auden's elegy exhibits a different kind of concern, that of Yeats's fate as a person and, in turn, the effect that this could have on his legacy as a writer. Unlike the poet that Shelley summons "Who in another's fate now wept his own," Auden is not motivated by his own fear of the critic's "barbéd tongues." Instead, his "mourning tongue" is far closer in intent to that of Dante, the poet by whom Auden chose to be judged in his "New Year Letter" (1940).

In the seventh circle of the *Inferno* of Canto XV, Dante meets the charred figure of Brunetto Latini, his old teacher. Latini, like Yeats, had dictated a doctrine of literary fame in his lifetime, enshrining his own reputation in his book, the *Tesoro* (The Treasure), "nel qual io vivo ancora" ("In which I still live"). Dante assures the shade of his fallen master that his tongue ("mia lingua") will make his indebtedness clear upon his return to the land of the living. However, Dante never fulfills his promise beyond recounting the fact of it and the circumstances under which it was made, a tacit criticism of the hollowness of Latini's earthly aspirations. Auden's mourning tongue eschews Yeats's own attempts to ensure his enduring fame, and, as Lipking argues "When Auden wrote his *tombeau*, Yeats's own must have still been ringing in his ears, and intentionally or not, his argument responds to Yeats's at every point." Auden's mourning tongue was to prove persuasive. The "familiar compound ghost" that T. S. Eliot encounters on the cinder path in "Little Gidding" (1945) conflates the shade of Brunetto Latini with that of a chastised Yeats. Instead of speaking of the fame endowed by his earthly achievements the fallen master speaks of how: "I am not eager to rehearse / My thoughts and theory which you have forgotten. / These things have served their purpose: let them be." Instead, like Auden, the familiar shade envisages poetic endurance in terms of inheritability and modification: "For last year's words belong to last year's language / And next year's words await another voice."

This first section ends with Auden asserting an impoverishment of reception and convention. Auden depicts a diminishing readership of "A few thousand" who will remember the day of Yeats's death, "As one thinks of a day when one did something slightly unusual." As with the poet's initial "disappearance," Auden ends this movement by striking a note of strangeness rather than sadness. The section is sealed with a reassertion of elegiac convention—that of the refrain: "O all the instruments agree / The day of his death was a dark cold day." However, the convention is emptied of emotional import, since the mechanical devices merely record, rather than react to, the death.

One of the most striking aspects of "In Memory of W. B. Yeats" is the markedly different tone that Auden adopts in each of the poem's three sections. The addition in April 1939 of the short, second section, an apostrophe to Yeats, was fundamentally to alter the structure and possible interpretations of the poem. The first version, published in March 1939, offered up Auden's poetic voice in the *vers libre* of the first section in immediate opposition to Yeats's voice in the tetrameter quatrains of the final section. However, the second, newer section interposed between the two original parts mediates between Auden's and Yeats's poetic voices as Auden directly addresses the dead poet. This not only dilutes the direct contrast between the two poets, but also undermines many of the consolatory assertions that Auden had already made in the elegy's final lines. Crucially, the addition of this section offers the reader an insight into the way in which Auden read and reacted to himself, and reflects the catharsis of resentment expiated by his initial turn to elegy. As we shall see in relation to the poem's third part, Auden's self-censorship of the *Collected Shorter Poems* version of the poem is also revealing. The earliest version "In Memory of W. B. Yeats" first denies and then copies the dead poet. The middle section seems to have been generated out of the dialectic between the two. What it "resurrects" is not the figure of Yeats, but rather what Auden regarded as the fundamental and enduring essence of poetry. Thus the poem in its final form functions as a kind of trinity, embodying as it does firstly the voice of the son, and finally the voice of the father, the quarrel between the two making apparent in the middle and mediating section the spirit that imbues and outlives them both.

In this later interpolated section Auden makes Yeats approachable, puncturing the older poet's self-imposed imperiousness, describing him as "silly like us," far from being a poet seer. Auden writes of how Yeats's gift "survived it all," obstacles social, physical, and psychological: "The parish of rich women, physical decay, / Yourself." However, as Auden will later go on to speculate in his "Postscript" to "The Cave of Making" (1964) his elegy for Louis MacNeice, the poetic temperament may be born of such difficulties and temptations, rather than in spite of them ("many a fine / expressive line / would not have existed, / had you resisted"). Though "mad Ireland hurt [Yeats] into poetry," the poetry created out of this turmoil cannot alter anything: "Now Ireland has her madness and her weather still." Yeats's poems are just as unlikely to be able to change Ireland's weather as her politics: "For poetry makes nothing happen."

This is one of the most contentious and misquoted statements on poetry in the twentieth century. It has provided Auden's successors with a crucial point of engagement with his poetic legacy. Much depends on what Auden may have meant. In his poem "Letter to Walt Whitman" (2002), Mark Doty muses: "Is it true then, what your descendant said, / that poetry makes nothing happen?" However, in figuring Auden as Whitman's descendant (and, in turn, himself as a descendant of them both) Doty implies that poetry makes something happen by the way it inevitably influences succeeding generations of poets. Paul Muldoon looks beyond the bounds of the influence of verse upon other verse when in his poem "Anseo" (1980), he describes one of his school friends who has joined the IRA as "fighting for Ireland, making things happen." Yeats's romanticized version of the mythic age of Celtic heroes has, even if unintentionally, served propagandist purposes. To understand what Auden may have meant we must look beyond the resources of the poem to Yeats's own beliefs, Auden's other pronouncements, and the historical and literary contexts in which this startling assertion was made.

Auden was to expand upon the idea that "poetry makes nothing happen" twice in the year that followed the publication of "In Memory of W. B. Yeats." In "The Public v. the Late Mr. William Butler Yeats," the defense counsel informs the jury that, "art is a product of history, not a cause [...] it does not re-enter history as an effective agent," while in "New Year Letter" (1940), Auden asserts that "Art in intention is mimesis / But, realized, the resemblance ceases; / Art is not life and cannot be / A midwife to society." Auden's intention may have been to rebut the question that Yeats puts to his conscience in "The Man and the Echo" (1938): "Did that play of mine send out / Certain men the English shot." The play referred to is, of course, *Cathleen ni Houlihan* (1902). Muldoon inverts Yeats's logic in "7 Middagh Street" to reveal what he regards to be its inherent fallacy: "As for his crass, rhetorical / / posturing, 'Did that play of mine / send out certain men (*certain* men?) / / the English shot...?' / the answer is 'Certainly not.' / / If Yeats had saved his pencil-lead / would certain men have stayed in bed?" However, Stephen Gwynn's contemporary account of attending the first production of the play at the Abbey Theatre in *Irish Literature and Drama in the English Language: A Short History* demonstrates that Yeats's concerns in the "The Man and The Echo" were informed by contrition rather than conceit. Gwynn wrote: "The effect of 'Cathleen ni Houlihan' on me was that I went home asking myself if such plays should be produced unless one was prepared for people to go out to shoot and be shot." Consequently, it is clear that the inherent danger of the play had been recognized years before Yeats wrote "The Man and the Echo."

Louis MacNeice seems closest to the mark in his monograph on *The Poetry of W. B. Yeats* when he accuses Auden of protesting too much: "As was natural in a poet who had abruptly abandoned the conception of art as handmaid of politics for the conception of art as autotelic, [Auden] overstates his case." MacNeice avers that: "It is an historical fact that art can make things happen and Auden in his reaction from a rigid Marxism seems [...] to have been straying towards the Ivory Tower." In "Persuasions to Rejoice: Auden's Oedipal Dialogues with W. B. Yeats," Stan Smith takes us into further into the motivating psychology that lay behind Auden's turn to the Ivory Tower:

> By 1939 Auden shared a similar anxiety [to Yeats], for, as he veered towards pacifism, he had become more and more distressed (as his notorious rewriting of "Spain" later that year was to reveal) about his own propaganda role in sending men to commit "the necessary murder" on behalf of the Spanish Republic. The revised version of this poem "Spain 1937," the added date carefully dissociating the author from his past, was to appear immediately before the Yeats elegy as the first poem in a section of "Occasional Poems" at the end of *Another Time*.

In the light of these facts Auden's statement starts to look like wishful thinking. The "intellectual disgrace" that Auden refers to in the final stanzas of his poem may refer not only to the disgrace of Yeats's political sympathies, or of disgrace of the politicians who, in 1939, had led Europe into a "nightmare of the dark," but also, possibly, to Auden's own shame. Not only the shame of his own intellectual disgrace, but also of his actual disgrace, in the face of the accusations of cowardliness leveled at him after his decision to abandon Britain on the eve of the Second World War.

As MacNeice points out, there can be little doubt that poetry does make something happen. Indeed, there may be no better example of poetry making something happen than in the case of elegy: a poetic form traditionally enacted in order to effect the result of consolation. Elegy's agenda may have changed over the past century, but one of its defining features continues to be its purposefulness, be it in wrestling the laurels from the hands of a dead poet, as in the case of professional elegy, or making a political point, as in the elegies of the AIDS activist Paul Monette.

Even if we take Auden at face value, and accept that "poetry makes nothing happen" within the confines of "In Memory of W. B. Yeats," the reader still finds that the very statement of poetry's powerlessness makes something happen. Auden assertion inverts elegy's traditional inefficacy trope (the "false surmise" of Milton's "Lycidas") by implying that this may, in fact, be its greatest strength. It is the very powerlessness of poetry that exculpates Yeats, a poet who had based his poetic credo around his own self-perceived poetic potency. Auden had already asserted that the dead poet has no power over how his poems may be interpreted, but the question of interpretation is unimportant if poetry is not a productive "effective agent," but rather, as Auden thinks, a by-product of humanity that manifests itself as a mimetic process. Auden adopted and amplified the ambivalent tone that Yeats took in his elegies, such as "In Memory of Major Robert Gregory," and incorporated his advances in synthesizing the personal and the symbolic into his own poetics. In "On Being Asked for a War Poem" (1916), Yeats responds to the title's request by asserting that: "I think it better that in times like these / A poet's mouth be silent." Auden modifies Yeats's self-imposed "silence" inside a *tombeau* of his own contrivance by placing his word in the mouths of the living, realizing that poetry is a contingent and mimetic process, "a way of happening, a mouth." Poetry continues to exist, surviving "In the valley of its saying," long after the mind that conceived it has been extinguished and the mouth that originally uttered it has been silenced.

"In Memory of W. B. Yeats" takes a strikingly different tone and form in its final section and offers the reader an excellent example of the atavistic element often present in professional elegy. Elegy is in itself atavistic, born of the resurrection of an ancient form, and elegies for poets are often where this strain is most apparent. Critics have repeatedly and convincingly asserted that Auden echoes Yeats's voice in these stanzas. Lipking argues that Auden draws on Yeats's prosodic legacy, putting his "linguistic virtues to use" as "the broken, hesitant rhythms and urban images of the beginning are healed into daring, old-fashioned quatrains," while Sacks contends that in reverting to the "ceremonious slow march of Yeats's rhymed tetrameter quatrains" that Auden is "eclogically trying to surpass the looser, skeptical voice of the preceding two sections." However, according to this criterion he deems the poem to fail, at least to some degree, since he finds this final section to be "the least satisfying." Though "the opening voice of Auden" in the first section suggests "the terms on which he may succeed the figure he has mourned," Sacks argues that in the eclogically necessary third section, the "caricatured version of Yeats's voice," creates a kind of aesthetic indigestion and is ultimately included "at the cost of marring his poem."

Though Auden's form undoubtedly draws upon Yeats's verse, and in particular "Under Ben Bulben," the whole section reads like a palimpsest of voices and allusions. Auden echoes poets other than Yeats, and, crucially, places the words in Yeats's own cadences. Thus, Auden's elegy ends by apotheosizing the dead poet into the ranks of the "Great master," by making Yeats's poetic voice ventriloquize them. Indeed, by the time of "A Thanksgiving" (1973) Yeats has become a named member of the pantheon that Auden venerates. The first lines of this third section, "Earth, receive an honoured guest, / William Yeats is laid to rest," not only reconfigures the scattered poet so he may be buried whole, but also is a direct allusion to Tennyson's "Ode on the Death of the Duke of Wellington" ("Who is he that cometh, like an honor'd guest …"). Auden conflates the words of a dead man (speaking of another dead man) with the voice of Yeats. Thus Yeats is buried not only in the earth but also into a fitting position in the poetic canon. In excising Yeats's middle name Auden seems almost to divorce the poet from his poems by creating an alternative avatar, one of William Yeats the man rather than William Butler Yeats the poet.

The following three stanzas (culled from the *Collected Shorter Poems* version of the poem) incorporate Yeats into an inverse poetic pantheon, including Rudyard Kipling and Paul Claudel, whose personal "views" could have damaged their reputations as writers. However, this ignoble band have been, or will be, rescued by the action of time which: "Worships language and forgives / Everyone by whom it lives." Though Auden dismisses the importance of this statement in the next stanza by calling it a "strange excuse," Joseph Brodsky seizes upon it in his prose homage to Auden, "To Please A Shadow," as the most striking line of poetry that he had ever read. In 1964, on being found guilty of "social parasitism" at a show trail in Leningrad, Brodsky was sentenced to five years hard labor and exiled to Norinskaya in the northern Archangel province of (then) USSR.

A friend in Moscow thoughtfully sent him an anthology of English verse with which to occupy his mind. Brodsky confesses that he was, "intending to read Eliot [...] But by pure chance the book opened to Auden's 'In Memory of W. B. Yeats.'" This coincidental encounter was to be an epiphanic experience for the young poet and was to have a profound bearing upon his subsequent life and poetry:

> I remember sitting there in the small wooden shack, the peering through the square porthole-sized window at the wet, muddy, dirt road with a few stray chickens on it, half believing what I'd just read, half wondering whether my grasp of English wasn't playing tricks on me. I had there a veritable boulder of an English-Russian dictionary, and I went through its pages time and time again, checking every word, every allusion, hoping that they might spare me the meaning that stared at me from the page. I guess I was simply refusing to believe that way back in 1939 an English poet had said, "Time ... worships language," and yet the world around was still what it was.
>
> But for once the dictionary didn't overrule me. Auden had indeed said that time (not the time) worships language, and the train of thought that statement set in motion in me is still trundling to this day. For "worship" is an attitude of the lesser towards the greater. If time worships language, it means that language is greater, or older, than time, which is, in its turn, older and greater than space. That was how I was taught, and I indeed felt that way. So if time—which is synonymous with, nay, even absorbs deity —worships language, where then does language come from? For the gift is always smaller than the giver. And then isn't language a repository of time? And isn't this why time worships it? And isn't a song, or a poem, or indeed a speech itself, with it caesuras, pauses, spondees, and so forth, a game language plays to restructure time? And aren't those by whom language "lives" those by whom time does too? And if time "forgives" them, does it do so out of generosity or out of necessity? And isn't generosity a necessity anyhow? [...] I could go on and on about these lines, but I could do so only now. Then and there I was simply stunned.

It is often assumed that Auden excised these stanzas because of the reference to Paul Claudel, who had died in 1955. However, the case could also be made that the idea of time worshipping language was antithetical to the notion that poetry makes nothing happen. In choosing the latter over the former twenty-seven years after he had first set out to write his elegy, Auden seems once again to be willfully asserting poetry's powerlessness. However, Brodsky's stricken astonishment twenty-five years after Auden wrote his elegy would seem to prove incontrovertibly that time does worship language. Indeed, poetry turns upon this very fact, and nowhere is this more apparent than in elegy, particularly in elegies for the poets through whom language has lived.

Many have noted the obvious echo of William Blake's "The Tyger" in Auden's command "Follow, poet, follow right / to the bottom of the night." Though metrical similar, the line's import is informed by Dante's voyage into the underworld with Virgil. The command is intriguingly ambiguous. Though it seems likely that the "poet" addressed is Yeats, Auden could be instructing Yeats's successors, and possibly even himself, to follow in the dead poet's footsteps. Mendelson makes a case for Auden alluding to Milton throughout "In Memory of W. B. Yeats." He argues that this is particularly apparent in the poem's final section, where he asserts that Auden is echoing Milton's "baroque manner and metaphors." However, though Auden's "baroque manner" is undoubtedly atavistic, it could be argued that the figure of Shelley casts a far more apparent shadow over the elegy than that of Milton. Mendelson also posits that Auden's repeated references to tears in the final part of "In Memory of W. B. Yeats" allude to the tears of "Lycidas." Milton's lachrymal motif incorporates not only the "melodious tear" of the grieving, but also the tears of the lamented Lycidas, which are wiped "forever from his eyes," by saints at the close of Milton's elegy. Indeed, it is this obliteration of tears that leads, in the immediately following line, to the cessation of the shepherd's weeping and the transformation of the dead poet into "the genius of the shore." Yet the similarities with "Adonais" seem equally, if not even more, striking.

Shelley initiates "Adonais" by blending the tears of the writer with the tears of the reader in his first few lines: "I weep for Adonais—he is dead! / Oh, weep for Adonais! though our tears / Thaw not the frost which binds so dear a head!" Crucially, though these initial tears "thaw not" Adonais's frost-bound mind, Shelley establishes a vital trope, connecting tears and the melting of frozen thought and emotion, a motif that Auden will go on to rework in his elegy for Yeats. In the first section of "In Memory of W. B. Yeats" it is the landscape that is frost-bound rather than the figure of the dead poet. However, in the final section of the poem Auden's verse seems to incorporate and modify Shelley's lachrymal motif. Where "frozen tears" adorned the dead poet's funeral wreath in "Adonais," Auden describes how: "Intellectual disgrace / Stares from every human face, / And the seas of pity lie / Locked and frozen in each eye." Like the frozen tears of the treacherous in Cocytus, the deepest level Dante's Inferno, Auden denies his damned the catharsis of weeping. They too are guilty of a form of treachery in their "intellectual disgrace." Their (unshed) tears are not occasioned by the death of Yeats but rather out of (self) pity for the "nightmare of the dark" that humanity found itself in 1939. Accordingly, it is not the death of the poet that will release the pent up tears, but rather the survival of his gift:

> With your unconstraining voice
> Still persuade us to rejoice,
>
> With the farming of a verse
> Make a vineyard of the curse,
> Sing of human unsuccess
> In a rapture of distress;
>
> In the deserts of the heart
> Let the healing fountain start,
> In the prison of his days
> Teach the free man how to praise.

"Unconstraining" seems to refer more to the liberating influence that Yeats's voice may have on his successors, rather than to any unconstrained quality that his poetic voice may have had. Auden sees the true value of Yeats's voice in how he makes "a vineyard of the curse," harnessing "human unsuccess" into "a rapture of distress." It is through the enduring power of the dead poet's verse to catalyze despair into rapture that Yeats may release his readers' frozen tears and let "the healing fountain start." The image of the fountain also seems to owe much to "Adonais." Shelley refers to his elegy as a "fountain of a mourning mind," and envisages how at the moment of the poet's death:

> ... the pure spirit shall flow
> Back to the burning fountain whence it came,
> A portion of the Eternal, which must glow,
> Through time and change, unquenchably the same.

Both Shelley and Auden are fundamentally concerned not with the death of the poet but rather with the ongoing life of poetry itself. The poet lives on not only in the poems that survive his life, but also in the enduring "portion of the Eternal," that will animate his inheritors. It is this "transmitted effluence," which Shelley informs us, "cannot die / So long as fire outlives the parent spark," that Auden rekindles in his elegy for Yeats. Vitally, Auden rekindles not only the poetic voice of Yeats in this final section, but also those of Tennyson, Blake, Milton, Dante, and, most notably, Shelley. Thus "In Memory of W. B. Yeats" not only describes, both also demonstrates, the survival of poetry after the disappearance of the poet.

Yeats's legacy is not transmitted as he prescribed and proscribed, but rather by Auden's critical, yet admiring, elegy, which enacts the very elements of the dead poet's art that "survive" and presents his legacy in an inheritable form, free from his shadow. Yeats's reputation is thus restored and his poetic influence ensured, an outcome that had been denied him through his very attempts to guarantee it. For a poet's legacy is not set in stone, like the epitaph dictated by Yeats at the end of "Under Ben Bulben," or the tomb ordered by Browning's bishop at

St. Praxed's church. The poet continues to live in what others chose to take from him rather than in what he deigns to leave behind.

"Yeats as an Example?" and "Audenesque"

In a 1979 interview Seamus Heaney was asked: "How do you face up to Yeats?" He replied: "I don't face up to him, I turn my back and run." However, Heaney's poetry and critical essays demonstrate that Yeats's shade cannot be so easily evaded. Heaney was born on 13 April 1939. In the same month the three-part version of "In Memory of W. B. Yeats" was published in *The London Mercury.* The coincidence could be regarded as portentous. Auden's elegy takes issue with, and can be read as a key to, many of the concerns that have subsequently gone on to shape and inform Heaney's poetic career. Heaney repeatedly contents with issues such as what it means to be an Irish poet; questions if poetry has the power or, indeed, even the right, to influence the political situation; and muses upon the fate of the poet's words after death and the way in which those words may influence, intimidate, or be incorporated by following generations of poets. In an interview I conducted with Heaney at Harvard in October 2004, he described how Auden's elegy for Yeats, along with Milton's "Lycidas," function in the poet's imagination in a manner akin to a poetic "portcullis": though on first sight imposing and unassailable, such elegies also provide the inheriting poet with a possible means of ingress to the tradition. As we shall see, for Heaney, "In Memory of W. B. Yeats" has provided a way not only to address the death of the Russian poet Joseph Brodsky, but also to approach the vexed issue of Yeats's poetic legacy.

Yeats could be considered conspicuous in his absence from Heaney's poems. When asked about this aspect of his work, Heaney replied that he had repeatedly assailed the figure of Yeats in prose; in a further interview in November 2004 he elaborated on his feelings toward the poet he had so exhaustively been both favorably and unfavorably compared to, commenting: "Yeats is just like a mountain range in the offing, lying there, there's no way I can address Yeats in any way. It's like an English poet addressing Shakespeare, with Yeats it's like a finished deposit. It's perfect in the Latin sense, it's done."

Heaney's most extensive exploration of what he finds "exemplary in [Yeats's] bearing," can be found in his 1978 lecture "Yeats as an Example?" which was subsequently published in *Preoccupations* (1980). The title and epigraph of the collection are taken from Yeats's *Explorations*, while the title of the lecture is, of course, a querulous spin on Auden's essay of the same name:

> I have to say something about why I put the question mark after the title of this lecture. "Yeats as an Example" was the title of an appreciative but not ecstatic essay that W. H. Auden wrote in 1940, so my new punctuation is partly a way of referring back to Auden's title. But it is also meant to acknowledge the orthodox notion that a very great poet can be a very bad influence on other poets.

Yet whereas Auden used Yeats as an example, not an exemplar, Heaney goes on to mitigate what he regards as Yeats's potentially malign influence by examining the ways in which Yeats could be considered a positive role model for other poets. He argues that Yeats offers us a model of the "perseverance" and "slog-work" required to be a poet and is particularly impressed by his command of forms, and the way in which he "encourages you to experience a transfusion of energies from poetic form," in the process demonstrating, "how the challenge of a metre can extend the resources of the voice." Heaney goes on to illustrate this point in his conclusion by directing us to, and then quoting in full, Yeats's late poem "Cuchulain Comforted." As Heaney writes, "It is written in *terza rima*, the meter of Dante's *Commedia*, the only time Yeats used the form, but the proper time, when he was preparing his own death by imagining Cuchulain's descent among the shades." In a similar manner, Heaney was to go on to borrow the meter of Auden's "In Memory of W. B. Yeats." This was not, however, in order to address his own death, but rather to approach the shades of Brodsky, Auden and, ultimately, Yeats in "Audenesque: for Joseph Brodsky" (*Electric Light* 2001) a poem which appropriates Auden's formal emulation of Yeats in the final section of "In Memory of W. B. Yeats."

Brodsky died from a heart attack in New York on 28 January 1996. In the second stanza of "Audenesque," Seamus Heaney points out a fearful symmetry in this "Double-crossed and death-marched date," since Yeats and Brodsky shared the same death day. However, this coincidence is probably not what suggested the suitability of Auden's tetrameter quatrains to address Brodsky's death. Rather, Brodsky's life and the manner in which it was profoundly informed by Auden's poetry, and particularly "In Memory of W. B Yeats," appears to have prompted Heaney to borrow from Auden, lending from Yeats. In his lecture "Sounding Auden" (*The Government of the Tongue,* 1989) Heaney offers up Brodsky's prose writings on Auden as "thrilling evidence of what can happen when 'the words of a dead man' are modified 'in the guts of the living' and a poet finally becomes his admirers," yet perhaps a better example of this modification can be found in Brodsky's "Verses on the Death of T. S. Eliot."

Brodsky composed "Verses on the Death of T. S. Eliot" on 12 January 1965, six days after Eliot's death in London. The poem was originally published in Russian and first appeared in English translation in Brodsky's 1973 *Selected Poems* (translated by George Kline and with a foreword by W. H. Auden). In "To Please a Shadow" Brodsky writes of his realization that the structure and form of Auden's elegy for Yeats "was designed to pay tribute to the dead poet." In turn, Brodsky freely admits that "W. H. Auden's poem 'In Memory of W.B. Yeats' was a model for my poem, 'On the Death of T. S. Eliot.'" Consequently, "Verses" functions both as an elegy mourning the passing of a great Modernist forebear and as an homage to the as-yet-living Auden and the long-dead Yeats. The poem is the product of textual stratification, a cento borne of Yeats, Auden and Eliot's poetic legacies. It functions much like a vanishing point on what Brodsky would have called the "plain of regard," a place where the dead poets' concerns and poetics converge.

The elegiac agenda of "Audenesque" is, however, radically different from that of "In Memory of W. B. Yeats" and "Verses on the Death of T. S. Eliot." This is not, as in the case of Auden's elegy for Yeats, or Brodsky's for Eliot, a poem that crystalizes the moment of poetic inheritance between the dead poet and the elegist. Indeed, the main poetic relationship posited here is not that between Heaney and Brodsky but rather that between Auden and Brodsky. Instead, whereas the other poems in this chain of elegy addressed the shade of a poetic precursor, Heaney's elegy struggles with the death of a contemporary and friend. In a manner akin to what Auden admires in Yeats's "In Memory of Major Robert Gregory," the deeply personal is transmuted into the profoundly symbolic in "Audenesque," though Heaney "never loses the personal note of a man speaking about his personal friends in a particular setting." Vitally, this outcome is achieved through the appropriation and revivification of Auden's (and, in turn, Yeats's) poetic form.

The poem starts with an assertion of formal immutability: the iambic tetrameter march of the final section of "In Memory of W. B. Yeats": "Wystan's Auden's metric feet" that "Marched to it, unstressed and stressed, Laying William Yeats to rest." Auden's use of Yeats's meter gives Heaney a means of expanding on his prose description of, and demonstrating at first hand, the "transfusion of energies from poetic form." In doing so Auden's mediating elegy provides Heaney with a means of resurrecting Yeats's poetic legacy through a formal homage which avoids the anxieties of copying or denying that Auden had identified in "Yeats as an Example" and oscillated between in "In Memory of W. B. Yeats." Heaney asserts that "Repetition is the rule," borrowing not only Auden's form but also his frost-bound imagery ("Dublin Airport locked in frost"). Yet Heaney goes far beyond the frozen tears of Auden's elegy, or "the frost which binds so dear a head" in "Adonais," when he envisages Brodsky frozen in an ice so unyielding:

> [...] no axe or book will break,
> No Horatian ode unlock,
> No poetic foot imprint,
> Quatrain shift or couplet dint,
>
> Ice of Archangelic strength,
> Ice of this hard two-faced month,

> Ice like Dante's deep in hell
> Makes your heart a frozen well.

Unlike Auden's "healing fountain" or Shelley's "burning fountain"—both images of the enduring power of poetry—Heaney seems to envisage a loss so profound as to freeze over the wellspring of poetry. Yet on further consideration it seems that his concerns are personal rather than poetic, for in rhyming his assertion of loss with an image of the frigid wastes of Dante's Cocytus, Heaney, like Auden before him, demonstrates the ongoing life of poetry and the power of the held line. Heaney is not one of those Irish poets with "unremembering hearts and heads" that Yeats feared would succeed him in "Under Ben Bulben." Rather, "Audenesque" is a consummate act of remembering, as Heaney recalls not only drinks, jokes, travels and puns shared with Brodsky, but also the words, forms and cadences of his elegiac precursors. In his penultimate stanza Heaney inverts the very lines of "In Memory of W. B. Yeats" that Brodsky had seized upon as his poetic credo: "Worshipped language can't undo / Damage time has done to you." Brodsky's words may well endure your but, on first sight, this seems to be cold comfort to his bereft friend. Yet this inversion is couched in the very form that Brodsky had in mind when he rhetorically mused "isn't a song, or a poem, or indeed a speech itself, with it caesuras, pauses, spondees, and so forth, a game language plays to restructure time?"

In the final stanza Heaney looks beyond Auden's reconfiguration of poetic consolation to a far earlier elegiac antecedent: *The Epic of Gilgamesh*.

> Dust-Cakes, still—see *Gilgamesh*—
> Feed the dead. So be their guest.
> Do again what Auden said
> Good poets do: bite, break their bread.

Like Auden, Heaney demonstrates the survival of poetry after the death of the poet by placing loss within a literary matrix. Whereas "Adonais" offered Auden a consolatory template for mourning a poet,

Gilgamesh offers Heaney an example of how one might lament the death of a friend. This Ur-text of loss, dating from the third millennium BCE, is one of the oldest surviving narratives in human history and deals with some of humanity's most ancient concerns: mortality and mourning. Elegies, like the month of both Brodsky and Yeats's death, are Janus-faced, simultaneously casting back into the past and projecting into the future. Heaney's final stanza functions as a microcosm of this ratio, as he conflates the very distant elegiac past with the immediate poetic future. His final lines no longer seem to be addressed to Brodsky. Rather, he importunes not only Brodsky's poetic inheritors but also his own to break bread with the dead. The image and sentiment are taken from Auden's May 1969 poem "The Garrison," in which he suggests that thanks to "personal song and language," "it's possible for the breathing / still to break bread with the dead." Auden expanded upon this in an interview for Swedish television a few months later in September 1969. When the interviewer, Göran Bengtson, ask if Auden felt himself "to be part of a continuing literary tradition," the poet responded: "Yes, and the wonderful—the other nice thing about the arts, the invaluable thing about them, is that they're almost the only means we have of breaking bread with the dead."

In many ways this statement could be regarded as philosophical gloss upon the assertions that Auden had made forty-two years earlier in his elegy for Yeats. Poetry may make nothing happened, but the held line survives and endures, resonating in the creative imaginations of future generations of poets. Heaney goes yet further by suggesting exactly how this poetic communion may happen. His most immediate allusion is, of course, to the kind of textual transubstantiation suggested by Auden in his elegy for Yeats; yet more specifically, it is Heaney's formal appropriation of Auden borrowing from Yeats that enables him finally to break bread with his problematic precursor. For as Heaney explained during a speech at Galway Town Hall in April 1997, and was to repeat at a reading of his elegies for poets which took place at Harvard University on 31 October 2004, if "poetry is what we do to break bread with the dead […] surely rhyme and meter are the table manners."

II.
The T. S. Eliot Prize

The T. S. Eliot Prize in Poetry

This is not a critique of the prizefication of the poetry world nor is it a commentary on the desirability or otherwise thereof. Yes, prizes are subjective, superficial and partisan; often making impoverished poets part with "reading fees" they can ill afford. Such awards frequently seem to reward what is popular rather than original and are, by their very nature, extremely reductive. Yes, such prizes are also a vital part of the contemporary po-biz; they provoke debate and draw attention and, possibly most importantly, financially support creative endeavor. This argument will rumble on as long as there are poets and honors. Rather than rehash that old chestnut, it is my intention here to consider the winning entries of just one of the many available accolades: the British T. S. Eliot Prize in Poetry (Not to be confused with Truman State University's confusingly and identically named prize celebrating the native Missourian.)

This award was established in 1993 to celebrate the fortieth anniversary of the British Poetry Book Society, and named to honor its founder. It is bestowed upon which the panel of expert judges determines to be the best collection of poetry published in the UK in that given year. Since its inception only two American poets—Mark Doty and Sharon Olds—have won the Eliot. "Foul play!" goes up the cry, surely indicative of a British bias against Creative Writing programs in general and the very idea of "workshopping" one's poems in particular; but this anomaly is far more a function of the vagaries of publishing than any bias on the part of the judges. Only British publishing houses can submit for the Eliot. Consideration, therefore, is limited to the kind of heavy-hitting and already well-known American poets who can secure a UK publisher.

Certainly the transatlantic remit of the Eliot accords well with his own, very well-known poetic career, which I will rehearse here but briefly. Born in St Louis in 1888 and educated at Harvard University, Eliot first came to the UK to conduct graduate work at Oxford in 1914. The outbreak of the First World War prevented Eliot returning across perilous Atlantic waters to Harvard to defend his PhD thesis. While in the UK he married Vivienne Haigh-Wood. In her preface to Eliot's first volume of letters, Eliot's second wife Valerie quotes from private correspondence of Eliot's where he commented on his disastrous first marriage: "I came to persuade myself that I was in love with Vivienne simply because I wanted to burn my boats and commit myself to staying in England." Eliot eventually renounced his American citizenship and became a British citizen at the age of 39, abandoning the Unitarianism of his upbringing and embracing the high Anglicanism that inspired *Ash Wednesday* and *Four Quartets*. After a stint as a banker at Lloyd's in the City of London he worked for Faber & Faber in Russell Square in Bloomsbury. In that capacity he did much to shape the poetic landscape of mid-twentieth-century British poetry and the careers several of the UK's best-known poets—including W. H. Auden, Ted Hughes and Philip Larkin—were nurtured under his watch.[1]

Eliot died in London in 1965 and his ashes are interned in the church at East Coker, the small Somerset village from which his ancestors set out to the New World in 1669. The circle is complete. His recursive epitaph conflates the first and last lines of the "East Coker" section of *Four Quartets:* "in my beginning is my end, in my end my beginning." Another fitting epitaph could be taken from Joseph Brodsky's "Verses on the Death of T. S. Eliot." Originally written in Russian while Brodksy was still in exile, the poem is patterned on Auden's great transatlantic elegy for Yeats. Brodsky imagines a consolatory tableau with the nations of his birth and death united in their grief:

> America, where he was born and raised,
> and England, where he died—they both incline
> their somber faces as they stand, bereft,
> on either side of his enormous grave.

---

1. I used to walk past his old Faber office on Russell Square every day on my way to class as an undergraduate in the 1990s. The building, now a part of the University of London, is adorned with a plaque celebrating his work there. One day I plucked up the courage to go in and ask to see his office. The security officer opened his large building directory, leafed through it, slammed it shut and announced, "Sorry miss, no one of that name works here."

Eliot, then, is the perfect "genius of the shore" of transatlantic poetry; a talisman for the interdependence and cross-pollination of the American and British poetic worlds considered in this book.

Of all the baubles available in, at least, the British poetry world, the Eliot is one of the most sought-after and highly regarded. One of the completely unavoidable though totally reductive metrics to measure significance is, of course, money. The £20,000 bestowed upon the Eliot winner is, though, relatively and transatlantically speaking, small potatoes. It is certainly not as lucrative as the biennial Bollingen Poetry Prize, which at $150,000 is one of the best-remunerated awards; but the Bollingen is only open to American authors, whereas the Eliot allows for any poet published in the UK during that prize year. The Eliot is not as well-known as the eye-wateringly generous MacArthur "Genius" Award, but this too is only awarded to American citizens and residents. The MacArthur at $625,000 over five years is only beaten in terms of total amount by the Nobel Prize for Literature, which currently approaches nearly a million dollars in Swedish Krona. However, both the Nobel and the MacArthur are for authors in general and not, specifically, poets (though, of course, many poets have won). This is also the case with the $150,000 Lannan Foundation Award, which, like the Nobel and McArthur, does not accept external nominations. It does, however, consider the work of non-U.S. residents. The Ruth Lilly prize for poetry, administered by the Poetry Foundation, comes next with a not-too-shabby $100,000 awarded to the poet for outstanding achievement, but that poet has to be an American.[2] The Academy of American Poets' Wallace Stevens Award also weighs in at $100,000, as does the mid-career Kingsley Tufts Poetry Award. Again, those two require U.S. citizenship or permanent residence. The Pulitzer Prize for

---

2. The philanthropist Ruth Lilly had submitted several poems to *Poetry* magazine prior to her death in November 2002, none of which were ever accepted. Perhaps impressed with that esteemed organ's editorial integrity, she left them a $100 million bequest on her death, leading to the establishment of the cultural behemoth that is now the Poetry Foundation. I was writing a series of reviews for *Poetry* at the time and called the office in Chicago the day they learned of the gift. They were beside themselves with shock and delight. I think someone was squealing with glee in the background. It was one of the most cheering phone conversations of my life.

Poetry is a relatively measly $15,000 (five of these get doled out per annum however) and, again a closed shop for Brits. Ditto the $10,000 National Book Award for Poetry. The Guggenheim is a fellowship for ongoing creative endeavor rather than an award for published work and, again, Limeys need not apply. Of all the major U.S. poetry prizes, only the Lannan and the National Book Critics Circle Award are open to poets published in the U.S. but regardless of nationality or residence. Possibly the most egalitarian of the prizes, unsurprisingly, is based out of Canada. The C$65,000 Griffin Prize, "the world's largest prize for a first edition single collection of poetry in English ... or translated into English, by a poet/translator from any part of the world," to which they touchingly and modestly add, "including Canada."

This is by no means an exhaustive list of the many and seemingly ever-proliferating poetry accolades, but it does illustrate the difference of what is at stake between the U.S. and the UK and how British poets are, for the most part, cut out of the American competitive circuit. This, perhaps, accounts for some of the Eliot's luster, even given the relatively small amount of the prize money compared to those top-level prizes awarded in the U.S. In the first line of Lowell's "Words for Hart Crane" the poet laments the Pulitzers "showered on some dope." This is even all the more fitting when we learn from the notes Frank Bidart's compendious *Collected* that Lowell had originally entitled the poem "An Englishman Abroad." Better throw oneself on the tender mercies of the Canadians.

In the UK the only prize that approaches the Eliot in terms of illustriousness is the Forward prize. Established a year before the Eliot, the Forward Foundation offers an award of £10,000 for the best book published that year which, like the Eliot, is open to submissions from American poets too. (The Forward too, has its fair share of American winners, including Jorie Graham, Claudia Rankine and two transatlantic poets: Michael Donaghy, an American in London, and Thom Gunn, a Brit in San Francisco). The major difference between the Eliot and the Forward is that the judging panel of the former always consists solely of other poets. This is unusual (in an informal poll of my colleagues we could only come up with relatively minor awards, such at the $3,000 Poets' Prize or the $5,000 James Laughlin Award for a second book, that function in a similar manner) and further complicates matters when it comes to accusations of favoritism, back-scratching and bias. The prospective judging pool, when reduced down to fellow poets, can scarcely fail to be unhealthily small. There were dark mutterings the year the Eliot was awarded to David Harsent in 2014 for *Fire Songs*. Fiona Sampson, his colleague at the University of Roehampton, was one of the judges and had positively reviewed that and other of his collections previously. She was also one of the judges on the panel when Harsent got the Griffin from the lovely Canadians for *Night* in 2012.... Small world.

Certainly, the Eliot has attracted its fair share of controversy. In 2011 Alice Oswald and John Kinsella both withdrew their collections from consideration for the prize to protest the struggling Poetry Society accepting sponsorship from Aurum Funds, a British hedge fund. Oswald explained, "I think poetry should be questioning not endorsing such institutions and for that reason I'm withdrawing from the Eliot shortlist." The Poetry Book Society was subsequently wound up due to its financial difficulties and taken over by the deep pockets of the T. S. Eliot Society (huzzah, as Michael Caines, my old colleague at the *TLS* points out, for Andrew Lloyd Webber's musical adaptation of *Old Possum's Book of Practical Cats*!). Recently a brouhaha erupted over Cambridge University research fellow Sarah Howe's debut collection *Loop of Jade* winning in 2015. The UK's *Guardian* newspaper asked if Howe was "too young, beautiful— and Chinese?" after a snide anonymous piece in the satirical *Private Eye* magazine that asserted that Howe had won due to "extra-poetic reasons." A patronizing interview with Oliver Thring in *The Sunday Times* only inflamed matters further, provoking a full-on Twitter storm in reaction to such insights as, "her verse pummels the reader with allusion, scholarship and a brusque, six-formy [i.e., high-school] emphasis on her own intelligence." One wonders if he would've said the same of her colleague, the Cambridge don J. H. Prynne. Called upon to defend his views, the maligned Thring lamented, "This gentle interview with a leading young poet has led various deranged poetesses to call me thick, sexist etc." A diverting afternoon may be had by looking at the #derangedpoetess responses on Twitter. This is, though, nothing approaching the furor that ensued after the inaugural Bollingen in 1948 was awarded to Ezra Pound for the *Pisan Cantos*. The scandal was such that the awarding powers were snatched from the voting Fellows of American Literature at the Library of Congress and given, instead, to a panel of judges at the Yale University Library. Everything, including scandal, is bigger in America.

So with all due caveats, contingencies, allowances, excuses and apologies in place I would like to present, for your delectation and consideration, this series of entirely subjective micro-reviews of all of the past Eliot winners.

1. 1993, Ciarán Carson, *First Language: Poems*

This is an exhaustive and exhausting read; a vast, cacophonous referential array. The title points to Carson's already much-discussed fascination with language and sonic devices (try to find another poet audacious enough to rhyme "triskaidekaphobia" with "Wachovia"). His was one of the only families in Belfast to speak Irish as their own first language (his parents had actually met at Gaelic classes) and the collection echoes with Irish (the collection has an Irish epigraph and starts with a poem in Irish), English, Latin and so on. There are a series of translations of parts of Ovid's *Metamorphoses* and poems after Rimbaud and Baudelaire. However, little critical attention has been paid to that "first" part of the title and Carson repeatedly dwells upon primacy and the nature of the subordination of the secondary. "Second Language" (there's also a poem entitled "Second Nature") might as well be the collection's title poem, which starts with the birth into language of the baby Carson (shades of the start of *A Portrait of the Artist as a Young Man*) in which we read of the "Wordy whorls and braids and skeins and spiral helices, / unskeletoned from laminate geology," of the Book of Kells. All of the switching between 1s and 2s makes one think of binary computer language and Carson seems fascinated between the synaptic leap and the boundary (the oft-visited "checkpoint" between Northern and Southern Ireland) between things and in particular language and experience. In the case of the former, its inherent slipperiness (he uses the idea of Babel six times in the collection), and in the case of the latter, the comforting idea of affixing experience. For all of its polyglot welter the collection brims with images of fixity: the repeated images of stars by which to navigate, the clocks that tick, measuring time, throughout, the abecedaries that contain the mess of the spoken word; the comforting limit of (the 58) "Heinz Varieties"; and Bertrand Russell's "R-Set," which consists of all items "'describable in exactly eleven English words'"

The closest I can find to any clue in the collection as to how one might read it is in a poem titled "Latitude 38ºS." In which we read of one "Fletcher" (traditionally an arrow maker, here fashioning a writing quill) who cut his finger sharpening his quill while "trying to copy the *Inquit* page off the Book of Kells, as if it were a series of 'unquotes'. The way you'd disengage / The lashes of a feather, then try and put them back together." The idea of the quill is profoundly significant for Carson, akin to Heaney's pen in "Digging." The quill stands for the Daedalean task of writing ("A Daedalus was herring-boning feathers into wings, I was / The sticky, thumby wax with which he oozed the quills together") and images of quills feature as hederae in "*Opus 14*" and "Tak, Tak." This idea of "unquotes" also accords with the manner in which Carson approaches form. For example, the atomized "Four Sonnets" where each of the fourteen lines is a discrete "lash" that reads like one of Wallace Steven's "Adagia." But unlike the Fibbonaci-perfect smoothness of the easy-to-reunite hooks on the quill it is nearly impossible to zip language up together again once unpicked. We are left like the hapless Fletcher trying to put Humpty-Dumpty back together again.

2. 1994, Paul Muldoon, *The Annals of Chile*
Another Ulsterman! Okay, I'm going to lay a completely crackpot theory on you here. I bet Muldoon and Carson were in cahoots and in conversation in these two Eliot winners. Not, you understand, plotting over the prize itself; rather that these two collections, composed at roughly the same time or thereabouts have so many

uncanny correspondences that one can read them as companion pieces. Muldoon and Carson are, after all, close friends who once performed together in a band called "Upstairs in a Tent." The usual party line on *The Annals of Chile* goes something like this: the entire collection is "ludic"; "Incantata" = magisterial elegy and "Yarrow" = critics performing mathematical gymnastics to make the 100-page-or-so poem fit with Muldoon's own provocative definition of the poem as an "exploded sestina."

So let's get the obvious echoes out the way, the (to be expected) references to the Book of Kells and the translations from Ovid's Metamorphoses. Neither man can resist the idea of the "ultrasonic scan." We also find the same "black blotting paper" used by the Queen ("so nobody can read the mirror image of Her private / correspondence" in Carson, while Muldoon writes of "a Queen whose very blotting-paper / was black, black with so much blood on her hands.") Now on to the more enlightening correspondences. So, the arrow / quill fashioned by Fletcher pierces to the heart of this collection obsession with direction. Indeed, it is even verbally and visually embedded in the "Yarrow" of the collection's main poem. Muldoon loves a riddle (cf. "Why Brownlee Left"), and The Annals of Chile reads like a crossword puzzle where the solution is teasingly just beyond the reader's apprehension. The clue is set at the close of the second poem, "Brazil," where we read of how "it was O'Higgins who // duly had the term 'widdershins' [the unlucky counterclockwise direction] / and 'deasil' [the lucky clockwise] expunged from the annals of Chile." We have seen this idea of erasure before with Carson's repeated consideration of "Tipp-ex" in First Language. In Muldoon this straight downward pull is used to extrapolate how they must be in Brazil or "if not Uruguay, then Ecuador," for, "it must be somewhere on or near the equator // given how water plunged headlong into water."

The collection's final line describes another plunge headlong into water: that of a "trireme, laden with ravensara / that was lost with all hands between Ireland and Montevideo," in an ill-fated widdershins direction, westerly across the Atlantic. Carson, with his numbering compulsion, has already written of "some Byzantine trireme" and "an Ark or quinquereme." In Carson these vessels are metaphors for the human brain and Babel, but here in Muldoon, their freight is a healing balm. The ship is lost on its way to the New World on the 38th parallel, off the coast of South America that Carson wrote of, and it is here where Muldoon's hapless crew realize too late: "we'd rounded not the Cape of Good Hope but Cape Horn." In this way the *Annals of Chile* provides the reader with the conclusion that so evades the reader of *First Language*.

I rest my case, your honor.

3. 1995, Mark Doty, *My Alexandria*

Doty's third book of poetry was the first of his to also be published in the UK. *My Alexandria* was published in the US in 1993 and dedicated to his partner, Wally, who died from the complications of AIDS in 1994. Many of the poems in this collection (one of my very favorites in this list; in fact, scratch that: one of my favorites ever) are elegies for those already lost to the disease (such as "Bill's Story," about a very early AIDS patient) and grapple preemptively with, at least at that time, the fairly inevitable specter of approaching death in the wake of Wally's illness.

One of the poems I have taught the most in my career as a poetry professor is "Fog," a dazzling meditation in unrhymed couplets upon the blurring of the boundaries of personhood, of the breaking down of the divisions between self and other, effected by the AIDS diagnosis of the other half of the couple. He considers of how "blood is utterly without // an outside, can't be seen except out of context, / the wrong color in alien air, no longer itself." The collection throngs with these indefinite images of fogging, blurring and bleeding, and yet also shimmers with gloriously precise and ornate imagery, and "all the sheen artifice / is capable of" ("Chanteuse"). Doty's baroque tendencies are oft criticized but I delight in his poems' lacquered brilliance. In fact, one may find an excellent example of this in a poem entitled "Brilliance" about a dying man's goldfish: "bronze chrysanthemums, // copper leaf, hurried darting, / doubloons, icon-coloured fins / troubling the water."

Doty also interrogates our conventional modes of consolation and commemoration—such as elegies and monuments—finding them wanting and inadequate to the task of celebrating those killed by AIDS. His poem "The Wings," about the AIDS memorial quilt, often fashioned from fabric taken from the clothes of the dead, proffers an image of a far more homely and humane kind of pubic commemoration and therefore more powerfully affective. He reflects:

> An empty pair of pants
> is mortality's severest evidence.
> Embroidered mottoes blend
>
> Into something elegiac but remote.
> One can't look past
> the sleeves where two arms pushed
> against a seam, and someone knew exactly
>
> how the stitches pressed against skin
> that can't be generalized but was,
> irretrievably, you, or yours.

The last word of this collection is "inconsolable," and yet, at his best here Doty generates considerable consolatory power in his albeit contingent flashes of insight into the nature of life and loss. *My Alexandria* demonstrates the importance of moments of beauty wrought by music (Chet Baker's trumpet in "Almost Blue," a church organ overheard in "Lament Heaven"), art ("The Ware Collection of Glass Flowers and Fruit, Harvard Museum") and, of course, poetry itself. For, he asks, aren't "such moments" "answering the little human cry / at the heart of the elegy, / *Oh why aren't I what I wanted to be, // exempt from history?*" Doty demonstrates in *My Alexandria* that the gorgeous can be at least a temporary bulwark against unavoidable loss.

4. 1996, Les Murray, *Subhuman Redneck Poems*
In one of the rapturous blurbs that adorn the cover of this collection, Andrew Motion fawns: "praising Les Murray is as hard as praising

Seamus Heaney." I'd say I find it much harder to praise Murray, and qualify that with a confession: I have never liked his verse. The screeds of admiring criticism heaped on Murray's Australian *oeuvre,* frankly, baffle me. I find the experience of reading his poetry akin to being forced to spend the weekend looking after one's curmudgeonly, xenophobic, argumentative and understandably unmarried elderly uncle who sulks around in a undershirt. Murray is not oblivious to this, of course, hence the title of the collection. Self-knowledge doesn't make that poetic persona any more personable though. Reading this collection for the first time for this overview was, I admit, a struggle. In a profile of Murray in *The New Yorker,* Dan Chiasson identifies some of the poems in this collection (such as "Rock Music") as "Rant Poems," and argues that Murray's work has become more empathetic since a near-death encounter with a chicken bone in 1996. I do hope so.

The best poems in this collection are those that turn away from Murray's hectoring tendencies and toward depictions of his native outback landscape, as in "Dead Trees in the Dam," where, "a misty candelabrum / of egrets lambent before Saint Sleep—/ who gutter awake and balance stiffly off" (I must admit a mild fondness for other of Murray's poems of the natural world such as his excellent stretched sonnet "The Strangler Fig"). These are heavily outweighed by censorious poems like "A Brief History" though, in which Murray, once again, diagnoses "cultural cringe" (an Australian form of a cultural inferiority complex) and anatomizes, once again, "tall poppy syndrome" (an Australian impulse to knock down the successful): "We are the Australians. Our history is short. / This makes pastry chefs snotty and racehorses snort. / It makes pride a bloody poppy and work an export / and bars our trained minds from original thought."

I guess it rather depends on what you want from your poetry. As you can see from my rapturous review of the Doty, above, I'm a fan of the transcendent and redemptive. I love a bit of the elliptical and evasive (see Carson and Muldoon above too). I'm not even averse to outrage (for example, the work of Paul Monette) or even artful malice (cf. my esteemed colleague at the University of Houston, the wonderful Tony

Hoagland) but there has to be some sort of compensatory quality, aesthetic or moral or otherwise, so that the poem exceeds its initial motive force. Murray's poems fail in this and seem to dead-end into their own disgust, and his rage seems all the more unpleasant due to its impotence. Compare, for example Murray's "Corniche," with Philip Larkin's "Aubade," both poems of stewing in insomniac dread in the face of one's own mortality. In fact, Murray expressly encourages you to do so, as he echoes Larkin's "I work all day and get half drunk at night," in the first line of his poem: "I work all day and hardly drink at all." Give me the Larkin rather than the larrikin any day and while you're at it give Murray a drink.

5. 1997, Don Paterson, *God's Gift to Women*
This is a surprisingly charming read for a collection that wields together motifs as disparate as a train obsession with frequent acts of masturbation. It's also often laugh-out loud hilarious. Paterson manages to combine his unmistakable poetic voice with a remarkable range of registers. The full poetic regalia appended to this poem—epigraphs, prologue, envoi and notes—often seem to function like the emperor's new clothes as Paterson wryly undermines any inclination to the high falutin'. The epigraphs, one from a child's book and one from the notes from an abridged version of St Augustine's *City of God*, reveal a fine appreciation of the unintentionally ludicrous at both ends of the spectrum. The collection's "Prologue" further establishes this tension between the sublime and the ridiculous. The poet in the persona of the "cantor" loftily instructs his congregation, "Be upstanding. Now: let us raise the fucking *tone*.... My little church is neither high nor broad, / so get your head down. Let us pray. Oh God." That unpunctuated "Oh God" is definitely far more an ejaculation than an invocation.

The notes are as evasive as they are enlightening; we learn that "some of the poems take their titles from the stations of the old Dundee-Newtyle railway" in his native Scotland, but no elucidation or rationale is given about the timetable times attached to those station poems. Is the collection meant to be akin to a railway journey, with the poems between station poems the scenery flashing past? This seems to be what Paterson suggests in the "The Alexandrian Library; Part II: The Return of the Book"

> The new poem is coming along like a dream:
> this is the big one, the one that will finally
> consolidate everything. It is the usual,
> but different: a series of localized, badly-lit,
> paradigmatic atrocities seen from a train.

Trains careen around his poems operating on a number of imaginative levels; in "01:00: Rosemill" we read, nearly inevitably, of "my cock / the train," but Paterson is not unaware of the pervasiveness of this tick, acknowledging, "The ghost of your hangover thunders away / (like a train; this should go without saying)."

Though Paterson writes beautifully about longing he is far more a lust poet than a love poet. The sexual encounters in these poems (such as in "Buggery" and "Imperial") have little to do with emotion other than the clear-eyed understanding that desire is a state of diminishing returns. His poems are particularly compelling when he uses a kind of Scottish magical realism that dislocates time and imagines various miraculous materializations, such as in "The Chartres of Gowrie," where a Cathedral appears out of the blue in a field; the residents "stand dumb in their doorframes, all agog at the black ship moored in the sea of corn." Some of my very favorite poems in this collection—"Homesick Paterson, Live at the Blue Bannock, Thurso" and "Postmodern"—are in a deliciously expressive Scottish idiom conjuring up overheard conversations at a smoky evening at a ceilidh. The latter, in particular, made me cackle with laughter. I won't spoil the glorious punch line but I can say the title is unexpectedly apposite.

6. 1998, Ted Hughes, *Birthday Letters*

Of all of the collections on this list Hughes's *Birthday Letters* is probably the one that has garnered the most public attention. It was published in early 1998 before Hughes died of cancer later in that year and consists of a series of poems composed over thirty-five years, addressed to his dead wife Sylvia Plath. It was a sensation the likes of which is rarely seen in the literary world of the UK; it was, literally, front-page news.

The tragic facts of Hughes's personally disastrous but poetically inspiring marriage to Plath are well known: his infidelity; their separation in the fall of 1962; Plath abandoned in a bitterly cold flat in London with their two small children; all of these circumstances along with a life-long struggle with mental health issues leading to her suicide in February 1963. Though Hughes maintained a stoic silence about her death, he was frequently blamed for it, his readings disrupted by shouts of "murderer!" and his surname repeatedly chipped off her gravestone in Heptonstall (this event is recounted in here in "The Dogs Are Eating Your Mother"). Some took his silence to be a mark of the callous indifference with which they felt he'd treated Plath in life, so the publication of *Birthday Letters* was, in many ways, a revelation. Controversy raged: was this collection the self-pitying justification of a dying man? Though an utterly fascinating insight into Hughes and Plath's fraught relationship, were the poems, in fact, any good? Did it deserve all of the awards heaped on it (along with the Eliot, the Forward, the Whitbread and the British Book of the year)? Was the entire endeavor mawkish and in bad taste? Should Hughes ever have let these poems be published?

The poems cover their entire relationship in roughly chronological order: from the moment he set eyes on "A picture of that year's intake / Of Fulbright Scholars" (of which Plath was one), to the decades-long aftermath of her suicide. These apostrophes and epistles to Plath are often affectionate but also, sometimes, chiding and reproachful. Hughes casts himself as a helpless acolyte, drawn inexorably into Plath's self-mythologizing, "I did not know I was being auditioned / For the male lead in your drama." Hughes frequently stresses the fatedness of their union; on their first meeting at a party at "St Botolph's" he writes, "That day the solar system married us / Whether we knew it or not." Critics such as Marjorie Perloff have demonstrated how, in the immediate wake of her death, Hughes (in his capacity as literary executor) manipulated the poem order of Plath's posthumously published collection *Ariel* to make her suicide appear nearly inevitable. In Plath's original schema the collection ends hopefully on the word "love." In Hughes's reworked order it closes with the ominous and seemingly inescapable certainty that "fixed stars govern a life." Here Hughes still harps on those "fixed stars." "The Bee God" (a symbol for Plath's father) is "Deaf to your pleas as the fixed stars / At the bottom of the well," while in "A Dream" Hughes writes that the phrase was originally his not hers, "Not dreams, I had said, but fixed stars / Govern a life." In *Birthday Letters* Hughes does not give Plath the last word but the conversation conducted in these poems is, on balance, redemptive to them both. Though some of the poems wallow in wounded exculpation, for example Hughes's belief that "Your real target / Hid behind me. Your Daddy" ("The Shot"), he does eventually admit "I failed" ("Epiphany"). At their best the poems of *Birthday Letters* tenderly celebrate Plath's life and work and leave us in no doubt as to the profundity of Hughes's grief at her loss.

7. 1999, Hugo Williams, *Billy's Rain*

I have a first edition of Williams' *Collected Poems* from 2002 in which he has inscribed, "To Sally ... In memory of our night of sin." Such an event, I can assure the kind reader, never occurred. Yet, given Williams' rakish reputation after the publication of *Billy's Rain*, it seemed entirely plausible at the time of scrawling since at the time he was the Lothario of literary London.

The collection is a verse diary in fifty-one poems of an extramarital affair with a younger woman called "Carolyn." Williams freely acknowledges that the events described are based on real life and, in an interview, recounted his saintly wife Hermine's reaction to reading the book (they've been together since 1964): "She read it through in half an hour and laughed at one point.... And then at the end she said, 'Five years work, eh,' as though I'd been slacking somewhat." One marvels at her forbearance. The poems are a series of acutely observed vignettes that capture the progress of the affair, tracing the heady initial excitement of their first illicit encounters, the gradual souring of the novelty, and Williams' despair at their break-up when Carolyn becomes involved in a relationship with her boss.

One of the collection's most compelling aspects is how funny Williams' deftly amusing ironic touch can be. One cannot help joining Hermine in her chuckles and then feeling immediately ashamed for indulging and excusing the awfulness. The roguish protagonist of theses poems is a self-indulgent, self-pitying peacock of a man yet is endearingly aware of his own vanity and frailty. The pose reminds me very much of Jules Laforgue, the late-nineteenth-century French poet probably best known now for his influence on T. S. Eliot, and, in particular, the persona of one J. Alfred Prufrock. Unlike Prufrock, Williams doesn't agonize over if he should eat the peach, but like Prufrock he is extremely fretful about his "Haircut," which had been supervised by Carolyn, and now, he envies its obliviousness to their subsequent break-up "its innocence, its happiness, its peace."

Shades of the flâneur too in the friable artifice of poems like "Silver Paper Men:"

> Regency bucks and belles,
> they appear out of nowhere, for no reason,
> leaning by a bridge or balustrade,
> admiring a willow tree.
> Given over to reflection,
> they do nothing for a season, in pairs,
> while a butterfly waits in mid-air.
> That impossible basket of flowers
> says all there is to say about love
> in their shiny black world.

Vanity abounds in the collection's repeated images of mirrors and reflections, and formally too in Williams' repeated use of poems of two mirrored stanzas of equal length. This extended reflection on reflections reaches its apogee and is shattered in "Mirror History" when Williams admits, "Round about here I become aware of your / existence for the first time, that you might even / be alive, in the sense that I am alive, / walking around having thoughts about everything, / but keeping a pleasant expression on your face." This reminds me very much of Iris Murdoch's observation that "Love is the extremely difficult realization that something other than oneself is real. Love, and so art and morals, is the discovery of reality." Ultimately, this is the collection's greatest strength. For all of his infuriating yet disarming self-indulgence Williams reveals the reality of love that exists beyond selfish self-regard.

8. 2000, Michael Longley, *The Weather in Japan*
Longley broods out from his author photo on the cover of my Wake Forest edition of *The Weather in Japan* like the winner of the year 2000 Ernest Hemingway look-alike contest. The poetic persona of the Northern Irish poet too, shares something with Papa: the clarity of diction, simplicity of style and interest in subjects such as war and beasts. The collection's title is the first line of the brief but evocative title poem "The Weather in Japan / Makes bead curtains of the rain, / Of the mist a paper screen." Longley invokes comparisons between that small rainy island and his own, for example in "Birds & Flowers," "Two inky smiles on handkerchiefs tied for luck like dolls / Flapping where the window should be, in Ireland and Japan."

Longley predisposes toward brief forms (he's particularly adept with the sonnet). We find this tendency to the attenuated particularly in the collection's first part that considers creatures and their environments. These are austere, graceful nature poems in the (extremely popular) mode of Mary Oliver. Instead, however, of her redemptive and radiant moments of transcendence won from communing with nature, Longley inclines to the Lawrentian, where such encounters reveal the human in the equation to be wanting, for example in an encounter with a otter we read of Longley's "unforgivable shadow on the sand—."

The best poems in the collection are about the First World War. Longley's own father, born in 1896, fought in that conflict and he describes him and his brothers-in-arms in the heart-rending poem "The Moustache": "My father, aged twenty, in command of a company / Who, because most of them shaved only once a week / And some not at all, were known as Longley's Babies." Many of these are powerfully horrifying poems call to mind Wilfred Owen's famous observation: "My subject is War, and the pity of War. / The Poetry is in the pity," such as when we read in "The Horse," of the poor beasts, "Shell-shocked, tripping up over their own intestines."

The most abiding motif in the collection is that of quilts. These are not the gorgeous and ornamental "Cloths of Heaven" that Yeats writes of, "Enwrought with golden and silver light, / The blue and the dim and the dark cloths / Of night and light and the half-light." Rather, these are stitched from a darker thread, and Longley seemingly asks the shade of Yeats in "The Design," "How do you sew the night?" In "The Quilt" we read of the "tears in the quilt pattern repeating" in the quilt in Emily Dickinson's bedroom in Amherst (another fan of the brief and brittle). The homograph "tear," may be read both ways here (Elizabeth Bishop uses this world to similarly great effect in her "Sestina.") Of course, the initial reading will probably be lachrymal, and that fits with the elegiac tone of much of the collection, but the more significant, I think, is that of rending and mending. In this manner the quilts blanketing this collection function like a metaphor for Longley's work. His work structurally embraces small scraps, but these are all part of a piece that he invites us imaginatively to stitch together in one of the collection's last poems "The Waterfall," "If you were to read my poems, all of them, I mean, / My life's work, at the one sitting, in the one place, Let it be here by this half-hearted waterfall.... / Leave them here, on the page, in your mind's eye, lit / Like the fireflies at the waterfall, a wall of stars."

9. 2001, Anne Carson, *The Beauty of the Husband*
One of the slightly more humiliating of the many embarrassing moments of my life came in 2001 while I was working as an Editorial Assistant at the *Times Literary Supplement* in London. The poetry editor, the wonderful Mick Imlah, instructed me to contact the poet Peter Reading about a possible review. I felt awful, having just read Reading's *C*, a traumatic recounting of the experience of terminal cancer, since I was the one who had to inform Imlah of his old chum Reading's recent demise. Mick was extremely surprised and amused by this news, for Peter was extremely hale and hearty: his "illness"

was artful fiction. You know, poetic license and all. So much for the intentional fallacy and my academic qualifications.

Like Reading's *C,* Carson's *The Beauty of the Husband: A Fictional Essay in 29 Tangos,* blurs the border of poet and persona in this portrayal of a decades-long faithless marriage. Carson's invention of a "tango" formally affirms the question Yeats poses in "Among Schoolchildren": "How can we tell the dancer from the dance?" The more interesting question, though, is that which Carson poses twice; which dancer in the tango gets to take the lead and "How do people / get power over one another?"

The collection shifts unsettlingly from a first-person confessional mode in the first third to the third-person character of the beleaguered "wife" and undermines the very idea of the fiction the title asserts, "Fiction forms what streams in us / Naturally it is suspect." This dissembling is fitting for what amounts to a poetic treatise on, and interrogation of, truth. The most important relationship in this collection is not, however, between the poetic interlocutor and the faithless husband of the title, but rather Carson and the shade of John Keats.

Quotes from Keats provide each "tango" with an interleaved epigraph and Carson is particularly keen to grapple with the Keats of that deathless equation, "Beauty is truth, truth beauty." Can one exist without the other? Carson tests Keats's hypothesis by making beauty a lying bastard. A mendacious plagiarist who "lied when it was not necessary to lie. / He lied when it wasn't even convenient. / He lied when he knew they knew he was lying." She also considers Keats's theory of negative capability (or as Carson has it in the title of Tango XVII "MAKING UP ONE'S MIND ABOUT NOTHING") asking what happens when uncertainty is bowdlerized: "You know Nahum Tate rewrote *King Lear* in 1681 and his improvements took the form (besides a happy ending) of reducing occurrences of the word *if* from 247 to 33." Contingency too in Carson's repeated revisiting of Keats's self-dictated epitaph with images of writing on glass and water; for example, our moral history is, "almost neat as mathematical / propositions except written on water." In the end this collection demonstrates that, "Love is not conditional / Living is very conditional."

10. 2002, Alice Oswald, *Dart*
In this collection Alice Oswald traces the flow of the River Dart in Devon from where it bubbles up in a marshy spring high up on a remote part Dartmoor until in floods into the sea, freshwater mingling with salt, at the estuary's end at Dartmouth, "where my name disappears and the sea slides in to replace it." The poem takes the form of "water's soliloquy," as Oswald formally and verbally recreates the river as it eddies down its course, its various sumps, boils and turbulent caldrons.

This is, however, not just the singular voice of the Dart alone, others become intermingled with it over its course, for as Oswald explains in her preface, "There are indications in the margin where one voice changes into another. These do not refer to real people or even fixed fictions. All voices should be read as the river's mutterings." This aqueous chorus contains the voices of the drowned, most notably the "Jan Coo" of Devonshire legend who haunts the river. Present too are the voices that make their (legal and illegal) livings from the water: the poachers, the wool makers that use the river's water to dye the pelts, the sewage worker, the stonewallers and tinners that their materials from the Dart; the ferryman and fishermen; along with the voices of other people and creatures that live along its banks. Oswald conducted recorded interviews with the denizens of area (the acknowledgements lists, for example, "3 anonymous poachers"). Though Oswald stresses their fictiveness these passages ring with verisimilitude and, often, humor. A woolworker ruefully comments about the filthy state of raw wool, "Unfortunately sheep don't use loopaper," or, for example, this delightful exchange, "We're fisherman, Matt, we won't starve / Sid, we're allergic / to fish."

Oswald writes with amazing onomatopoeic vigor; the wool-spinning machine, "knocking throbbing bobbining hubbub," and the hurdling river a "jostling procession of waters, its man strands overclambering one another ... all these scrambled and screw-like currents / and knotty altercations of torrents." Her descriptions of the natural world are often quite stunning; a dragonfly becomes a "gypsy-coloured engines on my hand" while a swimmer dives down "underwater" which "is all nectarine, nacreous." We also come across gorgeous juicy Devonshire dialect words begging to be adopted like "slammicking" (ungainly), "shrammed"(cold), "bivvering" (shaking) and "spickety" (spotted).

Oswald's training is as a Classicist (her excellent 2011 collection *Monument* distills *The Iliad* down into its deaths and epic metaphors) and *Dart* features the expected Naiads and water nymphs. The most intriguing classical dimension that Oswald brings to bear on the Devonshire countryside, however, is her incorporation of the myth that Brutus founded Britain. John Milton had toyed with the idea of writing an epic *Brutiad* about exactly this subject before settling on the subject matter of *Paradise Lost;* in *Dart,* Oswald locates their landing place at Dartmouth: "There a goddess calls them, / Take aim, take heart, / Trojans, you've got to sail / till the sea meets the Dart." Thus the end of the Dart becomes the source of British nationhood. That is not all we have to give thanks to the river for, though, Oswald gives it a voice and in doing so reminds us of the awesome, "force that orders the world's fields / and sets all cities is in their sites, this nomad / pulling the sun and moon, placeless in all places."

11. 2003, Don Paterson, *Landing Light*

Donald does it again! Thus far he's the only poet to have snagged the Eliot twice, and deservedly so. This is far more serious collection than the delightful *God's Gift to Women,* which won six years previously. This collection does speak to his earlier ones though as it picks up on his epic sequence "The Alexandrian Library" (part I in *Nil Nil* (1993) is concerned with a quest to a massive shop selling obsolete texts; part II, in *God's Gift* the writer in the library struggles with his postmodern epic and returns home defeated). Here in the third installment we read of the long dark night of the poet's soul and the onset of dawn where, "the twins are still sleeping, since this is a poem."

The dark night is of midlife Paterson *nel mezzo del cammin di nostra vita.* Dante's dark wood echoes throughout. There is, for example, an interpretation of Canto XIII of the *Inferno* where the Paterson personaggio encounters the Forest of the Suicides, Pier delle Vigne transmuted into an unnamed Sylvia Plath here (her "Winter Trees" provides the epigraph to the poem, and, as we shall see she is a perfect interlocutor due to her obsessions with twins and twinning). The main movement of this collection however, is not into the depths and darkness of judgment and uncertainty but rather into the "clear air" and speculation and flight. Paterson repeatedly uses the Scots word "lift" for sky and this exactly captures the feeling in may of these poems that dwell on, play with and redouble concepts pertaining to the airborne. This interest is, of course, indicated in the book's title, and we find poems of aviation, such as "The Black Box" and "The Landing." Flight is not just limited to planes, though, and we also find the angelic in "The Long Story," and the avian, such as the poor doomed fulmars of "St Brides: Sea Mail," their flammable secretions as valuable as Moby Dick's tallow.

In his *ars poetica* poem "A Talking Book" (the poem's couplets functioning like the recto and verso of the book) the book rebuts: "the Academy's swift and unannounced inspection: / this page knows nothing of its self-reflexion, / its author-death, or its mise en abîme. / Relax! Things are exactly as they seem." One would do well to ignore the book's advice since the unifying themes of the collection are exactly those of implied authorial death, repeated reflections, and an eternity of endless mirroring and twinning. There are Paterson's own twins, Jamie and Russell, the addressees of a pair of fine sonnets, "Waking with Russell" and "The Thread." Twins too in Zeus's "Letter to the Twins," Romulus and Remus, the paired "Twinflooer," and a twin parallel earth in "A Talking Book" though, the book warns, "You never meet your underself, other / than in dreams and sickness." Yet Paterson seems to confront his underself repeatedly here; for example, in "The Hunt," in which, when he finally confronts his quarry, revealed to be his own mirror self, "my hand hit the glass." The collection ends with Paterson aloft in "The Landing," where he "saw the complex upper light / divide the middle tread, / then to my left, the darker flight / that fell back to the dead." In the "early morning sun" Paterson realizes he doesn't have to chose between the dark wood and the landing light: "No singer of the day or night / is as lucky as I am / the dark my sounding-board, the light / my auditorium."

12. 2004, George Szirtes, *Reel*
One of the most substantial (in every sense) of the Eliot prizewinners, Szirtes's *Reel* is an impressive and extended contemplation of memory and loss. In particular, the poet probes how poetic form can be used to capture and commune with past experience and lost people and places. Szirtes came to England at the age of eight after his family was forced to flee their native Hungary in 1956, an event he describes in "My father carries me across a field": "Lost figures who leave only a blank page / Behind them." Many of the poems in this lengthy collection attempt to recapture his lost Budapest. The poet dedicates the collection "To the ghost of a childhood and the body of the adult," and *Reel* considers, if, as Wordsworth says, "The Child is father of the Man."

Szirtes has a commanding grasp of fixed forms and, especially, rhyme, which is used to great effect here as the city spools out in front of us in *terza rima*. This form is extremely difficult to execute in English (due to the relative scarcity of end rhymes compared to its Italian native habitat) but Szirtes's rhymes never seem forced or infelicitous. *Terza rima* is, in keeping with the collection's title and repeated references to films and filming, the most cinematic of forms, each interlocking stanza like a series of connected film frames. Of particular note among these engrossing tercets is "Meeting Austerlitz," in memory of W. G. Sebald. The dead writer takes on the persona of his own fictional creation in the poem, Austerlitz, the exiled orphan, who, like Szirtes, is looking for his identity.

Szirtes excels (much to my delight as a lover of formal poetry) in other fixed forms too: sonnets both English and Italian standing alone and in sequences, a sestina ("Elephant," in which Szirtes picks some fiendishly difficult end words to work around) and "Winter Wings," a concrete poem that inverts the effect of George Herbert's "Easter

Wings." The effect of so much formal ingenuity makes one aware of the solidity and substance of the verse in contrast to the often fleeting and vague subject matter of lost memories and locations. Early on in the collection Szirtes asks, "What hope for rhyme when even childhood calls / on fiction for an echo"? He answers this throughout Reel with resounding affirmation on rhyme's part. For rhyme is essential to recollection, as Szirtes so impressively demonstrates in "Mnemon," where memory dead-ends into the poem's couplets, which pair the same words together. Rhyme and meter recreate not only memory but the experience of time too, enabling one to recapture and contain the fleeting moment, for as Dante Gabriel Rossetti wrote, "The sonnet is a moment's monument." *Reel* is full of such monuments and the final sonnet of the sequence, "Turquoise," brilliantly demonstrates the temporal effects of poetry that the sonnet itself describes. For, Szirtes writes, "The Shakespearian ending which turns round / to claim your immortality in words / performs a gesture." That gesture is a stay against, and answer to, the onslaught of time.

13. 2005, Carol Ann Duffy, *Rapture*

After reading the first few poems I thought, perhaps, this collection of love poems charting the course of a doomed affair might just not be quite my cup of tea. After all, I've made a career of writing about poetry concerned with death, not love, but as I read on I became convinced of its awfulness. Duffy is currently the British Poet Laureate and, as I have discussed elsewhere in this book, that chore can have a deadening effect on any poet's output. However this collection was published years before she ascended to that particular throne, and, is, in my humble professional opinion, tedious dross. It's almost hard to criticize since there's very little of significance or importance to unpick and unpack. As Gertrude Stein said of Oakland, "there is no there there."

The poems are stunning in their mediocrity and their capacity for uninspired cliché. It's a lesson in how tepid hyperbole can be; a nursing home for dog-eared diction ("my soul swoop[s]," "the trees wept and threw away their leaves"), exhausted metaphors ("my heart

/ soft mulch / for a red, red rose"), and tired rhymes (light / night is repeated throughout; compare this with Szirtes's night / ammonite). This frequent recourse to an extremely limited palette of poetic devices is cloying, and at times Duffy is so hackneyed she seems close to parodying herself in these moon-lit, star-studded, river-banked, tree-shaded poems, in which all that is precious becomes transmuted into "gold" (I counted eleven separate instances before giving up). Even when Duffy strikes upon a moderately original image she can't help flogging it to death. In "Haworth" we read of, "The bleached dip in a creature's bone's your throat" and then a few poems later in "Elegy" we find, "this bone here / that swoops away from your throat." Her tick of trite repetition rings particularly hollow; in "Hour" "Time hates love, wants love poor, / but love spins gold, gold, gold from straw"; in "Snow" "light, light"; in "Answer" "yes, yes"; in "Write" "love love love," etcetera, etcetera, etcetera.

About a third of the mercifully brief collection is framed in sonnets and sonnet-shaped fourteen-line forms. Indeed, Duffy unwisely encourages comparison to previous love sonnets in a series of strikingly obvious allusions. Here is Keats's "Bright star" in her "December"; here Elizabeth Barrett Browning's "let me count the ways" and Donne's "O America" in "The Love Poem"; and here, inevitably, Shakespeare, the mistress's eyes of Sonnet 130 making a repeat appearance in "Whatever" and "The Love Poem." One might hope this familiarity with the greatest hits of sonneteering might've helped Duffy construct her own but to no avail. In "Art" we read of how love on its expiration is consigned to "art's long illness," enshrined in paintings or "fizzled into poems." Quite.

Duffy got in hot water in 2011 with Geoffrey Hill, the then Oxford Professor of Poetry, after she opined in an interview in the *Guardian* newspaper that "poems are a form of texting.... it's the original text." Hill disagrees, saying that he "would not agree that texting is a saying of more with less, and that it in this respect works as a poem." Yet this is exactly the trap that these poems fall into. They rarely amount to more than the sum of their extremely limited and meager parts.

14. 2006, Seamus Heaney, *District and Circle*

As a Londoner who used to take the green and yellow District and Circle Line each day to go work at the *Times Literary Supplement* offices in Wapping, it had never occurred to me how evocative the name of an Underground line could be. Of course there is precedence in John Betjeman's poems of Metroland, but that is to be expected from the quintessential poet of middle England and suburbia. What is the great Irish bard doing on such quotidian and British turf?

Perhaps Heaney was drawn to take his title from the line, since its combined colors are close to those that make up the Irish tricolor flag. Certainly the Underground cannot fail to suggest the chthonic and there is catabasis in "To George Seferis in the Underworld." More likely, though, is the fittingness of the circular and recursive route that the Circle Tube line takes and the idea of place denoted by the District Line, for the poems here are located, for the most part (with brief jaunts to Iowa and Iceland), in the landscape of Heaney's childhood. The only poem set in London is the title poem itself, a series of five meditative sonnets on a Tube ride that perfectly captures the experience, "As sweet traction and heavy down-slump stayed me. / I was on my way, well girded, yet on edge, / Spot-rooted, buoyed, aloof." The word "district" features solely in "Tall Dames" a prose poem detailing the travelling "gypsies" that would land "in the district" of Heaney's home in Mossbawn.

Far more significant to Heaney, then, is the Circle of the title. Circularity is structurally apparent as Heaney revisits the loci of his youth (for example in "The Aerodrome") and characters from his schooldays ("Senior Infants"). Circularity too in revisiting poetic subjects: the anvil of *Door into the Dark* (1969) in "Midnight Anvil" and we revisit "The Tollund Man in Springtime," in which Heaney describes himself "Lapping myself in time" as he revisits this figure from *Wintering Out* (1972). Most poignantly, the final poem of the collection "The Blackbird of Glanmore" revisits the subject of his four-year-old brother Christopher's death (the subject of "Mid-term Break" from his first collection, *Death of a Naturalist,* in 1966).

This poem exemplifies the kind of completion brought about by the recursive action of the poems in this collection. Of course the place is extremely familiar, and the collection is dedicated to Ann Saddlemyer, who rented and then sold the cottage at Glanmore, described here as "my house of life," to the Heaneys. We've seen the blackbird before in Heaney's work in "Kevin and the Blackbird." Here, the bird, singing on the lawn when Heaney arrives at Glanmore, is a consoling presence, its song bringing Christopher to mind, "A little stillness dancer— / Haunter-son, lost brother—/ Cavorting through the yard, / So glad to see me home." The poem recounts how one of the Heaneys' neighbors had taken a blackbird hanging around the family farm to be an ill omen before his little brother's death. Here the bird is rehabilitated and celebrated, a symbol of circularity and the power to be had in returning to the source:

> Hedge-hop, I am absolute
> For you, your ready talkback,
> Your each stand-offish comeback,
> Your picky, nervy goldbeak—
> On the grass when I arrive,
>
> In the ivy when I leave.

15. 2007, Sean O'Brien, *The Drowned Book*

This is only one of two books to win both Eliot and the Forward prizes for poetry for the same collection (the former is announced first in January, and the latter in September). The title comes from Prospero's promise to, "drown my books," and though we can find saturated tomes ("English poets, all gone damp / With good intentions, never read") and frequent images of drowning, this is a work that owes far more to *King Lear* than *The Tempest* (see Jen Hadfield's collection below for the latter). We join O'Brien on a bleak and blasted heath here, both pre- and post- apocalyptic, perched on the abyss between World Wars II and III.

Now, I like to wallow in a bit of gloom as much as the next scholar that specializes in elegy, but I found *The Drowned Book* a bit too crepuscular and nihilistic even for my morbid tastes. The collection's first half is completely sodden with poems about various bodies of inland water: rivers, estuaries, meres, drains. The great post-industrial rivers of Britain take on a particularly ominous cast, the Tyne becomes, "where the world / / Is beginning and ending," the Ouseburn at Newcastle (where O'Brien teaches at the university) becomes a "curdled trench," while the River Hull is full of "drowned dogs, drowned tramps." At the start of Joseph Conrad's *Heart of Darkness,* Marlow muses, "nothing is easier ... than to evoke the great spirit of the past on the lower reaches of the Thames." It might be easy but O'Brien doesn't indulge in it; rather, he evokes the decay of Britain's nineteenth century industrial legacy (the sewer system, the railways) and the terrible promise of the future on the reaches of the rivers of the North. The effect is intentionally oppressive.

The gloom is not entirely unrelenting; there are occasional moments of levity such as "Of Rural Life," but even here humor is extremely black. The poem in its entirety reads: "Pigs. Chickens. Incest. Murder. Boredom. Pigs." The best poems in the collection are those that harness O'Brien's polemical and diagnostic leanings to dystopian ends. For example, "Song: Habeas Corpus" is about thought crimes, "for in our time the future tense / will be the major threat." "Timor Mortis" is a rollicking catalogue of death, framed in the manic couplets of Louis MacNeice's "Bagpipe Music" (in which O'Brien audaciously rhymes "tits" with "Clausewitz"). The lament here is not confined solely to the makers, as in William Dunbar's great fifteenth-century poem, and the living and the dead are slung alike into death's gaping maw: "Donald Rumsfeld, Richard Perle, / Madonna and the Duke of Earl." Clearly the fear of death doesn't confound O'Brien; rather, it compels him as he invites us, "Come now, and board his empty ark—/ What need of poems in the dark?" O'Brien is particularly good in a poem on the legacy of Communism, "Proposal for a Monument to the Third International," in which we find, "Putin in his sheet-steel chariot," "brandishing a grail of blood and vlaast." One wonders if O'Brien in 2007 would've suspected Putin would still be at it eleven years later. His poem on Thatcher "Valedictory" is excellent too, an anti-elegy that speaks ill of the dead, of the "true blue Clausewitz," who, "Let the

General Belgrano, / S[i]nk to save our sheep, our guano" in the 1982 Falklands War with Argentina.

Perhaps O'Brien is much possessed by death because, as he writes in "Transport: after Stefan George," "Friends' faces, that greeted me lately, / Are gone into the dark." There are several excellent elegies for poets, including ones for Barry MacSweeney, Ken Smith, Michael Donaghy and Julia Darling. Particularly fine is a sonnet for my beloved "Thom Gunn," in which O'Brien writes of how, "We loved and feared your eager solitude, / The city as a man-made absolute, / A sunset grid of immanent desire." The collection lightens somewhat toward the end (Rilke's angels make an appearance) and we end in "Arcadia." However, the world of this poem is far from Sidney's utopia. Rather, the protagonist is condemned to be cast adrift on the "black waters of the lake" in, "an iron coffin," endlessly. I imagine the sensation must be akin to reading this collection repeatedly.

16. 2008, Jen Hadfield, *Nigh-No-Place*
The title poem of this ludic collection takes Caliban's drunken entreaty to Stephano and Trinculo to follow him to Propero's island in *The Tempest* as its epigraph. Like Prospero's, Jen Hadfield's isle is full of noises too. These poems are set in an array of remote locales: Alberta, Manitoba and, further north, Artic Canada. Hadfield's poetic voice really comes into its own, however, when contained by small islands, specifically the Shetland Islands (where she lives), rather than the vast expanses of the tundra.

These poems are full of whimsy and surprise; snapshots of Hadfield's life on the distant, rainiest fringe of the British Isles. The poet isolates and heightens her keenly observed vignettes with a painterly precision. For example in "Still Life With the Very Devil," plates are "stacked like vertebra. / Under the broiler, / turned sausages ejaculate." Acute attentiveness too in "Ladies and Gentlemen This Is a Horse as Magritte Might Paint Him," "from the creased Jupiter of his arse / to the spotted dominoes of his teeth." There's particularly something magical about the manner in which Hadfield conjures up her visions of her home islands, compared to the "Narnia No Moose" of Canada, which proves sadly devoid of Elizabeth Bishop's sacred beast, "Alberta's a miserable monochrome—/ a bootcamp of little brown birds, / no moose, / the grey, grey grass of home."

Like Bishop, Hadfield's considerable descriptive powers, and her talent for apt and original metaphor, are at their sharpest when writing about animals and the collection abounds with beasts. In "Canis Minor," a dog's tongue "spools out his head like magma." The "Prenatal Polar Bear" is suspended in his formaldehyde jar "like a softmint or astronaut / dreaming in his moonsuit— / a creased, white world. // His paws are opalescent and dinted with seedclaws." A hedgehog drunkenly picked up by Hadfield is like, "a kidney flinching on a hot griddle, or a very small Hell's Angel." My favorite, though, the limpet of "*Denouement*" that, "budges / a devastating millimetre."

There is something sacred in these observations of animals and, indeed, this collection does have a distinctly reverential dimension to it. This is particularly fitting for poems that are born out of the Shetland landscape since the remote islands of the UK—like Lindisfarne and Iona—have, traditionally always been sacred spaces. Hadfield frequently borrows from the language of worship (cadences of prayer and the Bible echo through "Thou Shalt Want Want Want") and the various characters and stories of world religions. Krishna makes an appearance as do Adam and Eve, while Buddha's lotus is transformed on the Shetland Isles into a "Cabbage," "cool leaves creaking—a Northern Lotus." However, these are profoundly secular poems. "Nearly a Sonnet" uses the first line from Edwin Morgan's assertion in "London," "There is no other life / and this is it," as its epigraph and redoubles the message by shouting it in all caps in the poem: "THERE IS NO OTHER LIFE. / It is in heaven as it is on earth." But be not afeard, for Hadfield shows us such a glorious vision of the Shetlands that we don't yearn for a prelapsarian state or heavenly reward, wonders enough are to be found here.

17. 2009, Philip Gross, *The Water Table*

The Eliot judges, though comprised of a different panel of poets every year, seem inordinately fond of collections based in, on or around water. In this case it is the broad Severn estuary that separates England from Wales (where Gross lives) that provides this collection's central image. Of the other collections that take the fluid as their overarching theme, this is, in my opinion, the best of the watery bunch.

The title is characteristic, and O'Brien brings a series of epistemological musings to bear on the vocabulary of the fluid, the resonances and philosophical possibilities of concepts such as "watershed," "catchment," and "meander." Like Seamus Heaney, Gross is fascinated by the concept of the "offing" which he explores in a series of interpolated poems titled "Between Land" He's particularly interested in the strange visual effects and disruptions that occur around and on water, for example "The Moveable Island," which "keeps its distances. Its reticence. Whichever / shore you look from, it seems to closer to the other." Heaneyian too is O'Brien's "Ice Man Dreaming." Like Heaney's bog people, he is a "befitting emblem of adversity," or rather stupidity in this case, his "grand slow downhill slalom," accelerated by climate change, "Old leathery foetus, // he's hundreds of years before term."

Gross's liquid vision in *The Water Table* is far more extensive that those of Oswald in *Dart* (circumscribed by the course of but one river) or O'Brien in *The Drowned Book* (circumscribed by noisome post-industrial dread). Gross takes the Severn estuary as a starting point (not naming it, though, until the final poem "Severn Song"), but widens his perspective to encompass the many and varied possible manifestations of the water that is central to our very existence. Most obviously (and unlike Oswald and O'Brien), Gross imaginatively sails beyond the mouth of the Severn to consider the sea that covers some seventy-one percent of our globe. "Atlantis World" considers what would happen if one day the "The unplumb'd, salt, estranging sea," of Matthew Arnold's "To Margeurite: Continued," just decided it's had quite enough of humanity and retreated, "like an Ice Age instituted overnight." He envisages the international fracas that would ensue as nations struggled to mark their borders without the sea to define their boundaries. Gross's nightmarish vision of an "Elderly Iceberg off the Esplanade," presents us with the horrifying prospect of a globally warmed iceberg floating inland after it "jumped ship from the loosening Atlantic." Though this "wasn't the last," O'Brien warns us, the elderly Iceberg is, "a message from last-ness, a crumpled / brown parcel from an unsuspected / awful aunt who might // just turn up any day to stay."

Most compelling, though, are Gross's repeated interrogations of the idea of the "body of water: water's body" ("Betweenland I"). Unlike Oswald's polyvocal and haunted River Dart, or O'Brien's stinking Northern trenches that run like scars across his dystopian landscapes, here Gross personifies water and anatomizes its parts, its "mouth" that "debouches—all our secrets" (Betweenland IV) and, then, in "Betweenland VII " not a mouth but an ear, / / the estuary's battered pewter hearing-trumpet / amplifying distance." He reminds us too, that we are writ in water, the bead of sweat that runs "from the corner of the eye down my cheek / to the tip of my tongue, just a drip // of the litres per day that rain down through us" ("Salt") and of how our fingerprints are "like tiny anticyclones, / googlied in off the Atlantic." Water memory may be physically impossible, but the concrete poem "Amphora" reveals the power of the memory of water functions homeopathically in our imaginations. How, like human memory, the wine seeping out of the sunken vessels, grows "by absence" and dilution "till each last molecule / in the ocean *knows / Itself* as Homer's / wine dark sea."

18. 2010, Derek Walcott, *White Egrets*

The Eliot was awarded to Walcott for this collection the year after a scandal broke out over appointment of the Oxford University Poetry Professor Chair. Rumor had it that the Eliot was awarded as a consolation prize (it was up against Seamus Heaney's excellent *Human Chain*).[3] This, however, does Walcott's elegiac and elegant collection, which was to prove his last prior to his death in 2017, a great disservice.

3. Walcott had been a frontrunner but was forced to withdraw himself from consideration after damaging allegations of sexual harassment of students by Walcott circulated in the media (it should be noted that these allegations had first been published in Billie Wright Dziech and Linda Weiner's 1990 book *The Lecherous Professor: Sexual Harassment on Campus.*)

White Egrets repeatedly returns to Walcott's Ithaca—St Lucia—and the motif of those rangy, graceful birds resonates throughout, "prompting the last word." He invites us to:

> Watch these egrets
> stalk the lawn in a disheveled troop, white banners
> forlornly trailing their flags; they are the bleached regrets
> of an old man's memoirs, their unwritten stanzas.
> Pages gusting like wings on the lawn, wide open secrets.

The rhyme of "egret" with "regret" sets the tone of these poems, preoccupied with aging, errors, failing powers, dead friends and lost loves; his fears of "my gift abandon[ing] me like the woman I was too old for." The idea of memoir is apposite too: after the 1992 Nobel Prize a certain *froideur* descended upon his work; but here, aside from occasional lapses into the refuge of the third person, Walcott is remarkably confiding and direct. Those flags are characteristic of this work too and frequently appear as indicators of the ambitions of empire. Also apparent here, one of this collection's only weaknesses: Walcott's love of a metaphor that takes the act of writing as its vehicle. He drives that one into the ground.

As is often the case in Walcott's *oeuvre*, the collection take the form of a numbered sequences, with subsequences ("suites" and "series") within. The effect is of a complex formal armillary, worlds within worlds. The first sphere for Walcott, though, is always the Ithaca of his beloved St. Lucia, where he is, "content as [Patrick] Kavanagh with his few acres" in Ireland. Walcott reflects on the significance of his island's namesake, "patron saint of isles and eyes, for my lack of vision!" Walcott repeatedly writes of his aging: of his diabetes and the blindness born of it, of how he's now racked, "by a whimsical bladder and terrible phlegm," a ludicrous Quixote figure tilting at lovers, trying to be, "Superman at seventy-seven." Walcott undertakes a pilgrimage to Sicily, the place of St. Lucy's birth, but instead of the saint's aegis he seeks a young woman with whom he, "a grizzled satyr" has become obsessed. The adoration is unrequited and unconsummated, "there was no 'affair,' it was all one-sided," but this adoration enables Walcott to both regret his past failings ("I treated all of them badly, my three wives") and exercise his considerable poetic powers.

The pilgrimage to Sicily prompts thoughts of another former resident, "the Sonnets and Petrarch," but these poems always seem to be just slightly too short or slightly too long to attain the comfort of sonnet status as they chafe against the imperialism of form. The poems are self-reflexive too in their treatment of elegy. The bougainvillea, "whiten and freak like Queen Anne's lace" a polarized image of the "pansy freaked with jet" in Milton's "Lycidas." Walcott worries that unlike the "pastures new" that Milton's monody promises, his "monody ... might deaden endeavor and envy." However, this collection abundantly proves that concern is unfounded. In this glorious swan song, rather than the bone-whiteness of Sylvia Plath (always a harbinger of abjection and erasure) here the whiteness of Walcott's regretful egrets is a reminder of possibility and forgiveness.

19. 2011, John Burnside, *Black Cat Bone*

This, along with O'Brien's *The Drowned Book*, are the only collections thus far to win both the Eliot and the Forward Prizes. I prefer it to the O'Brien, but I still don't think these dual winners are, by any the stretch, the strongest on this list. Like O'Brien, Burnside drags us into a profoundly unsettling and uncanny world. Perhaps I just don't like being perturbed in this manner.

Black Cat Bone is an immersive and subversive work that casts a dark spell as looks at primal, formative experiences and "the legends we made" to explain them. Burnside considers not only how fairy tales, old wives tales, parables and the Bible shape on our subconscious (how we are "HansChristianAndersened"); but also how we crave these tales to make sense of our emotions and order our experiences, thus enabling us to confront, "the grief / our stories prepared us for." The collection makes repeated references to Christian scripture, taking epigraphs from the Psalms, the Book of Judges, and the Gospel according to Matthew. We read of how if, "Go far enough, they say, / ... some hideous god / will meet you, like a shadow on the road; / go further still, and scripture closes in"

("Faith"). This is not the scripture of hope and consolation, however, but rather a hollow "Blunt Hosanna" and a "tatter of Hallejullah."

O'Brien frequently returns us to an infantile state here, recreating the childhood panic of being lost and to confront the bogeyman in the closets of various poems. In the first poem, "The Fair Chase," the young protagonist hunts a mythical beast in a wood, killing it, not heeding the folk wisdom that, "Everyone becomes / the thing he kills /—or so the children whisper." There is black magic afoot here too. Burnside's notes inform us that his collection takes its name from "a powerful hoodoo talisman," and the poem in which that bone is embedded—"Hurts me Too"—explores the connection between *eros* and *thanatos,* for when "*I love my love with an X,*" the kiss of love is also the X of obliteration. Love and death too in "The Day of the Dead," the "corpse-groom" and his "moth-eaten bride."

Burnside is particularly good at casting a dream-like spell in these poems (indeed, in one of his epigraphs, Franz Kafka says "*Bitte betrachten Sie mich als einen Traum!*" "please consider me a dream!"). His language has the associative logic of reverie, and many of these poems take place in the chimerical haze of the witching hours. One image to which we are continually returned in these moments is that of drowning. "Down By the River" is a poem from the perspective of a murderer drowning a woman, "She dies is a local flurry of dismay / as kittens do, held steady in a pail / of icy water." The epigraph of the title section picks up on a thought expressed in the first poem in the collection about, "the curious pleasure of the doomed, as they go under." Here Burnside quotes from Leopardi's poem "L'infinito," "*E il naufragar m'è dolce in questo mare,*" ("drowning in this sea is sweet to me"). In poems such as "Fair Hunt" and "Pieter Brueghel: *Winter Landscape With Skater and a Bird Trap, 1565,*" Burnside disconcertingly reveals us to be close to being dragged under, since we are skating over the surface of our life on very thin ice, "It seems a fable and perhaps it is: / We live in peril, die from happenstance, / a casual slip, a fault line in the ice."

20. 2012, Sharon Olds, *Stags Leap*

In this collection Olds plumbs the shallows of her misery. It charts the course of her separation from her husband who, "had come, in private, to / feel he was dying, with me," and leaves her for another woman, in etiolated detail. One is rather astonished to discover that there was anything "private" at all in the marriage, for, as Olds admits in "Left-Wife Bop," "he did not give / his secrets to his patients, but I gave my secrets / to you, dear strangers, and his too—/ unlike the warbling of coming, I sang / for two." One feels rather sorry for Dr. Olds.

The fundamental issue for the critic is that these aren't really poems. Rather one is dealing with relatively unmediated jottings that never climb clear of the wreckage of Olds's misfortune. They are embarrassing in their self-indulgence and, consequently, attempting to criticize these writings feels far too personal. Olds occasionally manages to aestheticize herself out of awfulness; "Left-Wife Goose" is a valiant stab at a nursery rhyme scheme. "Tiny Siren," this collection's best poem, recounts discovering a photo of husband's mistress in the laundry, "the photograph of a woman, slightly / shaped over the contours of a damp towel. / I drew it out—radiant square / from some other world."

These occasionally brighter spots, however, in no way compensate for the rest, which are, quite frankly, very bad. Some examples: in "Something That Keeps" we read of, "One two three / four five six seven eight nine ten eleven / thirty-two heads on the succulent throstle." In "The Easel" of Olds, "dis- / assembling one of the things my ex / left when he left right left," as if she's just learned about enjambment. Then there's the poetic diction so clotted as to be utterly risible, the, "Girdle of curdled pubic roots, / lumped breasts, husk-spouted nipples, / eyeballs with iris gone bazooka medusa." Generally, when the collection aspires to slightly more sophisticated poetic device, it is of the most obvious and overused sort, for example here in, "On the Hearth of the Broken Home," where she deploys the dreaded verbing the noun cliché, "jessed with its jesses, limed / with its radiant lime."

I was tempted to plead the Fifth over the whole sorry mess, recusing myself on the grounds of taste and decency, leaving this review unwritten, but then Olds did something so ghastly that I felt I had to say something: she appropriates 9/11 as an objective correlative for her pain. Of course, much critical ink has been spilled over Sylvia Plath's appropriation of holocaust imagery in "Daddy" and "Lady Lazarus." In the case of Plath, the counterargument goes, the aesthetic pay-off justifies the terrible cost (I'm inclined to agree in the case of "Daddy" but not in "Lady Lazarus"). Olds plunders 9/11 here with abandon and without even attempting to balance the books. In "Last Look," perhaps aware of her own awfulness, she places this act in the mouth of "a friend" who likens her need to see her husband a final time as in some way similar to, *"the families of / those who died in the Towers—that need to see / the body, no longer inhabited / by what made them the one we loved."* This would be appalling at best, but it becomes unforgivable in "September 2001 New York City," when she describes the day of her divorce at an office in the Chrysler Building. She's provocatively titled her poem to bring to mind the tragic events that took place that month, and then subsumes what happened into her own self-interested cause, describing, "the intact beauty of its lobby around us / like a king's tomb, on the ceiling the little / painted plane, in the mural flying." It's utterly disgusting to take the horrific deaths of thousands to stand for a symbol of one's minor, insignificant despair.

21. 2013, Sinéad Morrissey, *Parallax*

James Joyce used the idea of the parallax to frame the Circe section of *Ulysses;* Leopold Bloom and Stephen Dedalus's dual and differing perspectives of their shenanigans in Nightown intersect at various points in the narrative. Here, Morrissey's intent differs. She's interested in her own singular position and triangulates that according the acuteness of the angle at which one looks at events. Morrissey quotes from an early *Oxford English Dictionary*'s definition of "parallax" (where the emphasis is on a singular, rather than, as in later editions, dual perspective) as her epigraph to underscore this, "apparent displacement ... of an object, caused by actual change (or difference) of position of the point of observation." The only time the word is used in the entire collection is in relation to a singular point of observation in "Lighthouse," where she describes the "swingball of its beam," of how "it stands to catch / then hurls it out again beyond its parallax." Like that lighthouse and Emily Dickinson, she's interested telling the truth but most interested in telling it slant. In fact, in most instances here, that slant is the truth.

Morrissey's method is to take isolated moments—fixed in aesthetic aspic by photography, film, history, tapestry, painting and Mutoscope—and view them afresh from her perspective. She pays particular attention to parallax error, its tricks of distancing and foreshortening, with how it's "A Lie," "That their days were not like our days, / the different people who lived in sepia." She looks at this lie embedded in a variety of forms of representation—from puzzles and jigsaws to blogs—always digging away at the distance between verity and falsity. For example, in "The Doctors," she considers how photographs were doctored in Soviet-era Russia, of how "In this country / they are desecrating photographs—/ those that tell the truth of their own flown moment." This is particularly effective in the ekphrastic poems here that dwell on works of art that rely on the very idea of the slant as their central conceit: in this case Hans Holbein's painting *The Ambassadors* and Powell and Pressburger's film *A Matter of Life and Death*. I must admit bias at this point. The former, which resides in the National Portrait Gallery in London is one of my favorite paintings. The latter, one of my very favorite films. I am greatly indebted to Morrissey for revealing the fundamental correspondences between the two in, respectively, "Fur" and "A Matter of Life and Death."

In the glorious "Fur" Morrissey contemplates Holbein's masterpiece of the young (to our twenty-first century eyes at least) ambassadors. By the standards of the era, however,

> they haven't got long to go:
> the pox, the plague, the ague, a splinter
> in the finger, a scratch at the back of the throat

or an infection set into the shoulder joint
might carry them off, in a matter of writhing
hours, at any instant—

Rather than telling the truth straight and casting a "white skull straight," Holbein casts a skull obliquely in anamorphic perspective across their image as a *memento mori,* one that seems premature to our perspective but must've seemed imminently prophetic to his. Here Morrissey redoubles the parallax perspective—hers and Holbein's—and she does in "A Matter of Life and Death." The poem recounts her labor with her second child while, "the light is slant and filled // with running gold," spliced with scenes from the 1946 film. Powell and Pressburger were, like, Holbein, masters of perspective. As in *The Wizard of Oz* (1939) the shift in perspective is indicated through color, but whereas in *Oz,* "when / Dorothy / opens her dull / cabin door // and what happens outside is Technicolor" ("The Coal Jetty"), in *A Matter of Life and Death* heaven is a "monochrome: an anachronistic afterlife in grey," whereas life is in Technicolor. What connects the two realms together in the film is the slant of "a magical marble escalator—the original stairway to heaven." As Dickinson knew, "The Truth must dazzle gradually / Or every man be blind—" The slanting truth of Morrissey's *Parallax* is gradual and subtle and it is, undoubtedly, dazzling.

22. 2014, David Harsent, *Fire Songs*

This collection speaks to the main poetic preoccupations of Eliot himself, unlike any of the others on this list. It also reads like a counterpoint to Gross's *The Water Table,* that stresses the centrality of this particular element to our carbon-based lives, on a planet with a molten core, entirely reliant on the energy of the sun for our existence. This is *The Waste Land* for a post-Hiroshima world where "The Fire Sermon" takes on new and ominous significance. Harsent undoubtedly agrees with Robert Frost's appraisal in "Fire and Ice": "Some say the world will end in fire, / Some say in ice. / From what I've tasted of desire / I hold with those who favor fire."

Eliotic too are this collection's cast of characters; Harsent draws on mythical archetypes such as the witch (shades of Madame Sosostris) and the wise fool (who functions here much like Tiresias). We are also definitely in "rats' alley," where, in *The Waste Land*, "the dead men lost their bones." Rats multiply like, well, rats here in "Sang the Rat" and "Rat Again," for, as Harsent notes "the rat is ineradicable" and will survive, "the infinite rapture of the megaton strike, its head / slick with what it burrowed through, what fell, what kept it fed," while "You and I will close and fuse, bone seared to bone, flesh folded in" ("M.A.D. 1971 (Rat Run)"). There's even the brief, calm interlude of a "Death by Water" in "Dive." However, on reflection the incarnation of Eliot that most profoundly informs this collection is that of *The Four Quartets* in which:

> The dove descending breaks the air
> With flame of incandescent terror
> Of which the tongues declare
> The one discharge from sin and error.
> The only hope, or else despair
> Lies in the choice of pyre of pyre—
> To be redeemed from fire by fire.

Fire Songs riffs on and between these impossible dichotomies: between good fire and bad fire; fire at the beginning of the world and at the end; firelight and firestorm; regenerative fire or fatal fire; bonfire or pyre.

Harsent starts *Fire Songs* with the stunning "*Fire: a song for Mistress Askew,*" which combines the collection's major theme with its defining form. Song, after all, is extremely apt for a collection dedicated to the British composer, Harrison Birtwistle, that set Harsent's "Songs from the Same Earth" (included here) to music. Indeed this is a collection of poems so beautifully euphonious that on several occasions I found myself unwittingly reading them aloud. Anne Askew was a Protestant martyr tortured and then put to death at the stake in 1546. The poem recounts her silence under torture and depicts her horrific execution at Smithfield in shockingly vivid detail:

... that low rumble her blood at a rolling boil;
and what she screams from the centre, now, as her hair
goes up in a rush, as her fingers char,
as the spit on her tongue bubbles and froths, as she browns from heel
to head, as she cracks and splits, as she renders to spoil:
the only thing she can get to me through the furnace, as I lean
in to her, is *yes, it will be fire it will be fire it will be fire* ...

Mistress's Askew tongue declares and repeats that message throughout *Fire Songs* like the "Burning, burning, burning, burning" of the compound figure of St Augustine and Buddha in "The Fire Sermon." Harsent sets and feeds fires in our fevered imaginations. He takes us unblinkingly from *auto da fé* to atomic apocalypse until we reach the point of all-consuming imaginative flashover.

23. 2015, Sarah Howe, *Loop of Jade*

In *Loop of Jade* Howe considers "the obligation to return" physically and imaginatively to Hong Kong, the place of her birth, which she left along with her Chinese mother and English father before the British handed the overseas territory back to China in 1997. This is an unequivocally spectacular debut collection, full of glorious inventiveness and evocative detail, in which a dirty painter's palette becomes a "chewy rainbow, blistered jewels."

The epigraph is taken from Jorge Luis Borges's fictional encyclopedia *The Celestial Emporium of Benevolent Knowledge* by one "Dr. Franz Kuhn" that creates an absurd classification system for various types of beasts including, "belonging to the Emperor," "drawn with a very fine camelhair brush," and "having just broken the water pitcher." The quote is probably best known for Foucault's amused reaction to first reading it that he recounts in the preface to *The Order of Things*: "That passage from Borges kept me laughing for a long time though not without a certain uneasiness that I found hard to shake off." The unease stems from how the ridiculous any attempt to categorize, "the wild profusion of existing things." Howe uses this ludicrous taxonomy like an Oulipolian constraint and the collection features poems (among others) that take their titles from this list.

As previously discussed, it was, in some cases, Howe's very erudition that rattled some of those reviewing her work. This is condescending nonsense. She is a scholar-poet who wears her learning lightly but never pretends it doesn't exist. Why should she? She could be considered to be part of the Chinese scholar-poet tradition and she writes of this very lineage in "(k) Drawn with a very fine camelhair brush," which details how the Jesuits who first came to China believed the painted logogrammatic language to be "the lost language of Eden" and all the mistranslations and misunderstandings that ensued. For, like Borges's silly system, these slippages reveal "words' tenuous moorings" in reality. This is exactly what Howe explores in her poem "(e) Sirens" about her misunderstanding of the word "pickerel" in Theodore Roethke's "Elegy for Jane," taking it to mean a fish rather than a bird. Generative confusion too in "(h) The present classification" where the Sphinx's "riddle" also becomes "riddled," as in pierced and perforated. "(m) Having just broken the water pitcher," details how such homographs are enormously useful in circumventing censorship in present day China. We read of how the "anonymous blogger," "ponders how strange it is (how useful …) / that *I beg you for the truth* is pronounced / the same as *I beg you, Elephant of Truth!* // Or that *sensitive words* (as in filters, / crackdowns) sounds exactly like *breakable porcelain.*"

"The Loop of Jade" of the title poem is a baby bracelet a "pendent / ring of milky jade," that was given to Howe as an infant to protect her; and that qualifying adjective of imperfection is important. As sharp as her poems are, Howe is fascinated with the effect of blurring and obfuscating the boundaries, just as Borges and Foucault were. She repeatedly revisits what happens when the surface of language becomes "scumbled" ("Banderole"), to interrogate the relationship of language and meaning and to attempt to trace and make sense of her own Anglo-Chinese heritage, her "personal Babel: a muddle. A Mendel" ("(l) Others").

24. 2016, Jacob Polley, *Jackself*

What a delightfully transporting read this was. Polley and I are of the same vintage of Britishness and many aspects of the fantastical world of *Jackself* are recognizably that of 1980s England; a land of lime cordial, baked beans, digestive biscuits and, school lunches of, "cartilage stew and spreadable carrots / the flavor of warm steel tins" ("Lessons"). These elements from Polley's Cumbrian childhood are woven together with the otherworldly in this magical collection, which inhabits an uncanny alternative existence spun together from fragments of English folklore and myth. In particular the proliferating protagonist, the adolescent and protean Jackself, is the everyboy of English nursery rhyme, a place-holder name for endless versions of selves: Jack Sprat, Jack Frost, Jack O'Lantern and Jack O'Bedlam among other coinages and kennings such as Jackdaw, applejack, jackshit, Jackspan and skipjack.

The epigraphs (one from Gerard Manley Hopkin's sonnet "My own heart let me more have pity on," from which Polley takes the name of the title, and a quote from the anonymous poor "Tom O'Bedlam" mad song) point not only toward the collection's wandering quest-like structure to confront "The Misery," but also to its robust language and frequently atavistic and incantatory forms. Though the muscularity of Polley's language is, undoubtedly, influenced by Hopkins, his is a distinctly direct and northern voice that owes much to Basil Bunting and Ted Hughes too, "Jackself stamps his foot / and all the carp and sticklebacks, the perch and pike and bream / are shaken out / of their gullible, muddy-minded dream." After the inaugural poem, "The House that Jack Built," sets the stage for this particular realm by placing it in the context of arboreal time ("the first trees were felled / and sailed in, wrecked, then slept / an age in the northern sun"), a narrative sequence ensues.

This collection describes the relationship between Jackself and his best mate Jeremy Wren (apparently a descendant of Christopher, since he claims "his granddad built the southern domes") and the aftermath of Wren's suicide (who "choked his way into a box"). Wren and Jackself knock around "Lamanby" (an ancient Cumbrian place name that functions as a *locus amoenus,* like Basil Bunting's Briggflatts), getting into teenage trouble, "way out among the hedgerows, Jackself / and Jeremy Wren, drunk / on white cider and Malibu, / are kicking up dust, the froth / of the cow-parsley spunk" ("Les Symbolistes"). The conversations between the two often share the hilarious verve of John Berryman's Henry and Mr. Bones dialogues. In particular Wren ribs Jackself for his writerly pretensions: "A POEM! Wren roars / you're as creepy as a two-headed calf." As he comfortingly rubs the vomiting, alcohol-poisoned Jackself on the back he comments, "that's a proper poem for you / agony to bring up, / with real carrots in it." Those carrots from the authentically grim school lunch make me think of Marianne Moore's formulation for poetry, "imaginary gardens with real toads in them." The creation of an utterly compelling imaginary garden with "Jackself in his toadskin hat" is one of Polley's greatest achievements here.

After Jackself slays "The Misery" that consumes him after his friend's death, he strikes "The Comeback Deal," and pays "The Tithe" of language in a poem of erasure and redaction to enable him to reincarnate Wren (but he warns his dead friend that "it's not as if this is a Jesus-type / comeback deal ... this is not a resurrection situation"). We end with the wandering Bedlamite Tom (the name Bedlam hospital a bastardization of Bethlehem) of the epigraph becoming "Jack O'Bedlam" in the collection's final poem, an incantatory spell of reanimation and rebirth:

> I'm in the house of Bethlehem
> lying in a manger
> it's my turn then
> to turn again
> And meet myself a stranger

* * *

So there you have it, folks; every one of the twenty-four winners of the Eliot since the prize was established in 1993. A bit of a curate's egg with some outstandingly awful collections (I'm looking at you, Olds and Duffy) and some resoundingly marvelous ones (the Connolly Prize would go to Morrissey first, then Doty, then Howe). As partial, reductive and political as such awards are, they are nevertheless a necessary evil in the world of poetry. For anything which makes people pay attention to what Auden in "The Cave of Making" termed an "unpopular art," one which "cannot be turned into / background noise for study / or hung as a status trophy by rising executives, / cannot be 'done' like Venice / or abridged like Tolstoy, but stubbornly still insists upon / being read or ignored," is surely a very good thing.

III.
Transatlantic Traffic

Poems about Ezra Pound in Old Age

It's a striking fact that the poets of the Modernist movement were to write very few elegies. Yet though Modernist poets rarely, if ever, set out expressly to write an elegy, they often seem to have ended up writing poems that functioned in very similar ways. For example, Ezra Pound's "Hugh Selwyn Mauberley" and T. S. Eliot's *The Waste Land* could be considered deeply elegiac. However, if the Modernists were more elegiac than they may have initially seemed to be, they have proved extremely hard to elegize. The shadows their reputations cast have often struck their inheritors dumb with either reverence or rebellion. Pound, in particular, has suffered from the perception of inapproachability. And, of course, the reasons for this elegiac inhospitality are stronger in Pound's case than that of any other Modernist poet. For example, in his 1972 *Love and Fame* poem "The Heroes," John Berryman writes of the competing processes of influence that were at play in his developing poetic imagination between Pound, Eliot, Joyce, and Yeats. Pound, he felt was, "not fated like his protégé Tom or drunky Jim / or hard-headed Willie for imperial sway." Pound's fate, this lack of "imperial sway," is, of course, due to his fall from grace in the 1940s, and may go some way toward explaining the apparent reluctance on the part of those poets who followed him to elegize Pound.

I do realize the facts surrounding his disgrace are well known so shall only rehearse these briefly here: Ezra Pound was sixty years old when he was arrested for treason in Italy on May 3 1945. He'd started broadcasting propagandist and anti-Semitic lectures from Rome on behalf of the Italian Fascist party in 1941. After his arrest, he was initially interned in a cage at a detention camp near Pisa, which precipitated a nervous breakdown and provided Pound with the material of *The Pisan Cantos*. He was then extradited to the United States to be tried. However, Pound was deemed unfit to stand trial by a Federal jury due to reasons of insanity. He was incarcerated in St. Elizabeths Hospital in Washington, D.C., in 1946 and was to remain there for the next twelve years. It became something of a rite of passage for young poets to visit the master, and over the years many poets were to make a pilgrimage to see Pound in St Elizabeths, among them Charles Olson, Robert Lowell, Elizabeth Bishop, and Louis Zukofsky. In 1948 there was outrage when Pound controversially was awarded the Bollingen Poetry prize for *The Pisan Cantos*. The New York Times headline read "Pound, in Mental Clinic, Wins Prize for Poetry Penned in Treason Cell." He was finally released in 1958, whereupon, describing the United States as "a lunatic asylum," he returned to Italy, where he was to live until his death in 1972, just two days after his eighty-seventh birthday. He's buried in the graveyard on the island of San Michele in Venice.

Three poems about Pound in old age immediately spring to mind: Elizabeth Bishop's 1950 poem "Visits to St Elizabeths"; John Berryman's Dream Song entitled "Eighty" (a reference to Pound's age) published in 1969; and Robert Lowell's "Ezra Pound" (I'll be discussing the version from his 1973 collection *History*). Of course, with further investigation I discovered quite a rich seam of poems. However, these almost without exception avoid the conventions of the formal commemorative poetic elegy. Those poems that do address Pound's death sidestep the valedictory and celebratory by focusing on the site of his grave (for example, Clive Wilmer and Anne Stevenson both have poems entitled "At the Grave of Ezra Pound" and both of these place particular onus on the brevity of the lapidary inscription compared to the prolixity of Pound's literary output). Instead I found a series of conflicted homages that address themselves to the figure of the as-yet-living Pound, and in particular the figure of Pound in old age. Such poems are often keen to focus on locus and circumstance (such as Charles Wright's "Homage to Ezra Pound," a poem about visiting Pound in Venice, or Laurence Ferlinghetti's "Pound at Spoleto," a prose-poem that describes the elderly poet giving a tremulous reading at the Italian literary festival). Others focus on artistic representations of Pound, such as Jeremy Hooker's ekphrastic poem on the "Hieratic Head of Ezra Pound," which is the title of Gaudier-Brzeska's bust of the poet. Other poems focus on literary remains rather than the loss of the poet, as in Veronica Forrest-Thomson's poem on the "Letters of Ezra Pound" or Gavin Ewart's acerbic quatrain "T. S. Eliot and Ezra Pound,"

> Eliot loved the music halls
> (and he probably loved pantos).
> Pound took the rubbish out of *The Waste Land*
> and put it all into the *Cantos*.

I also found protest poems: contemporary and retrospective poems railing against Pound's incarceration at Pisa, (such as Robert Duncan's "Homage and Lament for Ezra Pound in Captivity" and Donald Davie's "Ezra Pound in Pisa"); poems protesting about celebrations for Pound (such as Donald Davie's "On a Proposed Celebration of Ezra Pound," which is actually a backhanded compliment that suggests that no celebration could be equal to Pound's poetry); and, in particular, interrogatory and accusatory poems protesting about Pound's release in 1958.

In an edition of *Commentary* magazine published in November of that year I found Paul Potts and Danny Abse's "Two Poems About Ezra Pound." In his poem Potts asks if Pound should ever be forgiven, asserting that, "The Crime was too big. / There are no extenuating circumstances. / You should have known better." Danny Abse's response to Potts's question about "extenuating circumstances" in relation to Pound distills down the issue facing those attempting in any way to redeem him in and through their poetry:

> Gentle Gentile, (Potts) you asked the question.
> Pound did not hear the raw Jewish cry,
> the populations committed to the dark
> when he muttered through microphones
> of murderers. He, not I, must answer.
>
> ...
>
> In the chromium bars they talked of Ezra Pound
> and excused the silences of an old man,
> saying there is so little time between

> the parquet floors of an institution
> and the boredom of the final box.
>
> Why, Paul, if that ticking distance between
> was merely a journey long enough
> to walk the circumference of a Belsen
> Walt Whitman would have been eloquent,
> And Thomas Jefferson would have cursed.

The three poems that we're going to look at now are all concerned with the extenuating circumstances, and in particular the "ticking distance" left to Pound in old age, and the final poem we'll turn to, Lowell's, lets Pound answer.

I'm going to first look at the only one of these poems written while Pound was still incarcerated; it's also probably the best-known poem about Pound, Elizabeth Bishop's "Visits to St Elizabeths." It became apparent to me while considering these poems that Bishop, Berryman and Lowell all focus on the location, be it a mental institution or Westminster Abbey. However, Bishop's is the only poem of the three that omits the presence of the author and the circumstance of the encounter with Pound. She adopts the form of a nursery rhyme—patterned on the expanding stanza form of "The House That Jack Built"—to formally suggest ideas about cumulative causation and to imply a sense of constructive culpability in relation to Pound and his ideas without ever having to explicitly state a judgment about him. And of course, unlike the other two poems, Pound is never named or identified within the poem.

Bishop juxtaposes the child-like innocence of a nursery rhyme scheme with a depiction of her visits to the imprisoned Pound over the years 1950–1951. Her adjectives suggest a tone of studied ambivalence toward the figure of Pound who is variously described as "tragic," "talkative," "honored," "cranky," "cruel," "busy," "tedious," and "wretched." The only time that we find two conjoined adjectives is when Pound is described as an "old, brave man" in the sixth stanza. In this yoking together of the concepts of age and heroism Bishop seems to agree with Pound's own depiction of old age in his 1909 *Personae* poem "In the Old Age of the Soul" in which the poem's speaker in old age "flame[s] again toward valiant doing." Yet this moment of nobility is at odds with Bishop's form which with its accreting lines suggests causality, and, consequently, guilt and blame.

Whereas Lowell and Berryman both place Pound in relation to themselves and to his greatest friend, T. S. Eliot, in their poems, Bishop rips Pound out of his poetic context and places him among the other inmates: a sailor, a boy, a soldier, and, most significantly a "widowed Jew." Again, Bishop's opinion is tacitly implied rather than overtly expressed. The limited cast of characters and their repeated manic actions, their dancing; winding; weeping; waltzing and patting along with the limited and muted palette of end words—Bedlam, man, time, watch, sailor, board, ward, hat, flat, floor, door, war—creates the effect of an exhausting lunatic whirligig of insanity and obsessive behaviors. Yet the obsession that led Pound to this place—his opinionated speechifying—is never given voice within the world of the poem. His talkativeness is merely mentioned but not described. Perhaps the repeated refrain "that lies in the house of Bedlam" nods not only toward Pound's internment but also his perceived verbal mendacity. However, this is not a poem that lets Pound, as Danny Abse would wish in his poem eight years later, answer. Rather it is a poem that considers what he called "the ticking distance," Pound's time served.

The idea of time appears first in the poem in the line "this is the time." By a process of prepositional accretion we learn that this is the time, displayed on the wristwatch of a sailor that "tells the time" to various incarnations of Pound. The last stanza leaves us with the image of "the crazy sailor / that shows his watch / that tells the time / of the wretched man / that lies in the house of Bedlam" as Pound's years in St. Elizabeths accumulate like the lines in Bishop's stanzas. This, of the three, is least exculpatory of the poems, but one is left with the sense of how arduous Pound's twelve years on the inside, from the age of sixty to seventy-three, must have been. However, Bishop is careful not to present this, as Paul Potts would have it, as an "extenuating circumstance," but this is exactly what Berryman does in his Dream Song for Pound, "Eighty" which describes Pound's attendance at T. S. Eliot's memorial service in Westminster Abbey in 1965. This is, of course, particularly poignant since Pound is attending the kind of public celebration for his closest contemporary that would, rightly, never be afforded him due to the opinions that he had expressed. There is, of course, no plaque in Poets' Corner for Pound as there is for Eliot. Berryman describes Pound thus,

> Lonely in his great age, Henry's old friend
> leaned on his burning cane while his old friend
> was hymnéd out of living.
> The Abbey rang with sound. Pound white as snow
> bowed to them with his thoughts—it's hard to know them though
> for the old man sang no word.

Again, as in Bishop's poem, Pound is denied a voice; however, Berryman does speculate as to what Pound might be thinking and contrasts Eliot and Pound's shared youth ("Gone them wine-meetings, gone green grasses / of the picnics of rising youth. / Gone all slowly") with Pound isolated and "Lonely in his great age." Indeed, this poem could be read almost as much as a premature elegy for Pound—"Dry, ripe with pain, busy with loss"—as a poem occasioned by Eliot's death, since Eliot is figured in the poem only as Pound's "old friend."

I was very struck by the odd image of Pound's "burning cane" in Berryman's poem, an image which suggest not only his frailty in old age, but also, I think some degree of purgation as it nods toward the close of Pound's "Canto 116" (pirated versions of these Cantos were available as early as 1967) and the appearance of "a light, like a rush light, to lead us back to splendour." I think this idea of purification can also be found in the repeated images of Pound becoming bleached-out and ashen in the poem. He is described as "white as snow" in the first stanza, an image elucidated in the final stanza: "White is the hue of death & victory." However, it is not Pound but rather time that is victorious in this poem. The bleaching action of time seems akin to that posited in Auden's elegy for Yeats, when Auden asserts (this is from the first version of the poem, he was to subsequently cut out these lines) "Time ... Worships language and forgives / Everyone by whom it lives." Indeed, we can see this very idea at work in the drafts of this poem as Berryman changed the last line of the second stanza, "only the traitor body failing," to the far less accusatory and far more pity-inducing "only the albino body failing." Berryman muses upon what Pound's last words might be, but it is his own last words that do the most to redeem Pound "all the old generosities dismissed, / while all the white years insist." Age has bleached out and appalled Pound's dangerous and passionate intensities. He is, in this poem, a figure to be pitied rather than judged. The passage of time itself has become a mitigating factor in the ongoing trials of Ezra Pound. The decades of old age in exile their own kind of purgatory.

This idea of purgation is expanded and named in Robert Lowell's poem "Ezra Pound" which takes us from his time "Horizontal on a deckchair in the ward / of the criminal mad" to his later years in Rapallo. Unlike Bishop or Berryman's poem, Lowell's finally gives Pound a voice, and incorporates two separate speech acts on the part of Pound in the poem, both indicated by the present continuous phrase "you saying." The first vocalization ("'... here with a black suit and a black briefcase; in the brief, /an abomination, Possum's *hommage* to Milton.'") locates Pound in the poetic tradition in relation to his old friend Eliot and takes place during one of Lowell's visits to St Elizabeths.[1] Significantly, this is in relation to a retraction of an earlier opinion on Eliot's part in relation to John Milton. Eliot had famously dismissed Milton as a "bad influence" but was to recant and soften his critical stance in later years. Here the incarcerated Pound regards this change in his friend's opinion as a weakness, "an abomination." In the second speech act Pound himself softens his own opinion on Eliot, mournfully asking, "'And who is left alive to understand my jokes? / My old Brother in the arts ... and besides he was a smash of a poet.'"As in Bishop's poem, Lowell incorporates the passing years, starting with Pound's release in 1958, "Then sprung," and then ten

---

1. In the personal mythology of their friendship, Eliot was the play-dead Possum, and Pound the wily and obnoxious Br'er Rabbit.

years spent in Italy up to 1968, three years after Eliot's death in 1965, in Pound's eighty-third year. This older Pound is in stark contrast to his earlier unyielding incarnation in the poem, and Lowell links this to the wisdom of age: "You showed me your blotched, bent hands, saying, "Worms. / When I talked that nonsense about Jews on the Rome wireless." Lowell gives the elderly Pound the last words in the poem, for when he asks him "who else has been in Purgatory?" Pound bitterly retorts "'I began with a swelled head and end with swelled feet.'"

Pound, of course, had attempted to create his own kind of Dantesque structure in the *Cantos,* moving through purgatorial states toward at least the possibility of the Paradisal, and the last lines of the manuscript "Coda" to the *Cantos* read:

> I have tried to write Paradise
>
> Do not move
>   Let the wind speak
>   that is paradise.
>
> Let the Gods forgive what I
>   have made
> Let those I love try to forgive
>   what I have made.

However, here we are left with an image of the physical purgation of old age (swelled feet) rather than Pound's poetic accomplishments (swelled head). Time may "worship language" as Auden suggests, but as Seamus Heaney writes in his elegy for Joseph Brodsky: "Worshipped language can't undo / Damage time has done to you." And ultimately all of these poems use Pound's age to some extent to distance him from and, to some degree, mitigate the mistakes that he made as a younger man.

It's not been my intention in any way to excuse Pound's opinions or actions but rather to explore the ways in which these poems and poets present age as a form of exculpation. Yet one of the most striking images I found in relation to Pound was in William Carlos Williams's 1927 prose and poetry sequence "A Folded Skyscraper," where he's described as "Pearly Pound," long before his literary legacy was contaminated by his political views. I think, for the poets I've looked at, this is how he functions in the poetic tradition: as the grit in the oyster, as a necessary inflammation in the world of poetry.

Two Interviews On Thom Gunn

1. In Conversation with August Kleinzahler

SC: I wanted to start by talking about your initial meetings with Thom and your initial correspondence. Because you wrote him a letter, wasn't that how you met?

AK: Yes. I went to see him give a talk on Basil Bunting at a little venue south of Market Street, probably later in the year I got here in 1981, and it was a wonderful talk. Smart, modest, appreciative, in all the right ways. I was surprised and impressed. I was prepared to be, what's the word, disapproving, because he was after all a Faber man, a London and a Farrar Straus Giroux poet. However—

SC: Now you are [an FSG poet].

AK: Now I am. He's also the establishment, and I was avant-garde and Bunting was avant-garde and he [a poet from the North of England] was my mentor, who disapproved of Southerners. But it was terrific. There was an editor, a young editor my age, and a wonderful poet from Berkeley named Jim Powell, whom I had met before. I'd seen Thom on the N-Judah [a tram line in San Francisco] so I knew he was in the neighborhood and I got his address from Jim Powell, and sent him a note, sent him my little Canadian book, *A Calendar of Airs,* and he invited me by for a drink. As he would later put it, it's not hard to get him to invite you over for a drink and meet, it's the second invitation that's difficult. But we got along. He greeted me, he was very striking-looking and in those days I guess he would have been about 50. He was wearing a sleeveless T-shirt, like a dark T-shirt, and he had very lurid tattoos on his arms, and tight jeans. He sat on the couch and sat very, very close by, plying me with cheap wine and marijuana. I was a little bit uncomfortable, but I've been in that situation before. He soon enough figured out that I wouldn't fall prey to his powers of seduction, as handsome and compelling as he was. Just the wrong gender.

And then he invited me back, I don't know if it was the next time or the time after, he invited Michael McClure who also lived in the neighborhood. He's also well-known, a member of the Beat Group. He was Thom's age, and also, like Thom, famously good-looking. He wanted me to meet another poet in the neighborhood. He's very generous that way. But I was sitting between them. They were both very vain, very handsome men. I mean, uncommonly so. They were talking about how beautiful each other was.... Michael was saying, "My wife thinks you're the handsomest poet in America." And Thom was saying, "Oh, you're much handsomer than me, everyone knows you're the most beautiful." There was a lot of wine and marijuana, and Michael brought some cocaine over.

SC: That might have had something to do with it, then.

AK: And there I was squeezed between them, sort of squeezed between these two guys talking about how gorgeous they looked. But it was sort of sweet, and they were both very kind to me. Michael I got to know through that introduction later; he also lived in the neighborhood. And then over time, incrementally, Thom and I got closer. He was a shy man, and English, after all; you know what they're like. So it was an incremental kind of friendship, but over time we became very close friends. It was a time when I was developing as a poet; I was just thirty-one. Thom was very responsive and helpful, attentive to my writing and my suggestions, and he was encouraging and suggested things to read. Also he was great fun. I mean, he was just a bad boy. It was like having a very naughty uncle, who happened to be very brilliant as a poet and intellectually brilliant. So we became pals, and it was one of the great friendships of my life.

When he died, you know, I was shaken and upset but not surprised, because I think he wanted to die, and he didn't enjoy old age. And the friendship had been so satisfying, there weren't really any loose ends. I'd wish he'd seen me become successful, or I wish this or that. No friendship is perfect; he had his difficulties and I certainly had mine, but it was probably the great literary friendship of my life. That it was with someone 20 years older and from a very different cultural background just seemed to make it more special.

SC: Can I ask you a question about that, as well as the mentorship aspect, because of course Basil Bunting was mentor to you, and then Gunn. It's quite interesting you've had both British influences, but then you're this profoundly American poet with this geographical awareness of your nation and where you are, and where your place is in it. Why did you think that these two British poets and in particular Gunn spoke to you so much, and how American do you think Gunn made himself? Because this is one of the aspects that I'm fascinated by, being a Briton who's come over here. I'm trying to understand his Americanization, and when I spoke to Mike Kitay (Gunn's partner), he said, well, he would have been delighted to have been thought wholly American. He wanted to assimilate utterly, and was that your experience?

AK: Yes, he loved the idea of America. He loved the idea of the outlaw, the motorcycle outlaw, Marlon Brando, and the wild child on the skateboard, and Elvis. But he was terribly English, and he would have been deeply irritated to hear me say so. But he couldn't wash that stain off. One of the things that's most interesting about his poetry is that not only is he an Elizabethan poet in contemporary guise, but he's a very English poet in American guise, though not self-consciously so. Auden was never taken with the American notion; it's not so evident in his poetry, and he's the closest thing equivalent in terms of it, an exotic species like Thom. Bunting was in the Modernist tradition, and his primary contemporary interest were Americans, Ezra Pound and his contemporaries that most interested him like Louis Zukofsky and to a lesser extent with William Carlos Williams. He was interested in British Modernists, like Hugh MacDiarmid and David Jones.

Thom latterly came to American Modernists on his move to the States, studying with Yvor Winters and really becoming introduced to poets like Williams and Wallace Stevens, who had a large impact on him. T. S. Eliot, with both Bunting and Thom, it was a different phenomenon. I had a high opinion of him, but Eliot's a different thing, an American who's ardently trying to sound British. My attraction to Bunting was that he was a Modern, although his great poem *Briggflatts* is very much rooted in his Northumbrian experience; there are a number of techniques going on, but his modernist approach to it appealed to me.

Thom's poetry didn't interest me at the point when I met him because I was still educating myself in the tradition as it related to twentieth-century British poets. But as I learned more and read more Elizabethan poetry, I learned to appreciate his achievement, which is considerable. However, I don't think he becomes an interesting poet until 1965 or so, 10 years after he's moved to America. I don't find his early books, particularly the first couple of books which gave him an enormous reputation in England, interesting at all.

SC: *Fighting Terms* caused quite a stir....

AK: Well, it's enormously accomplished, particularly for a young writer, and he's striking a tone and a posture which are very attractive, probably, at the time in Britain. I don't think it would have had that impact in the States.

SC: Well, he had that whole theory of posture in the poem as well that he writes about. Were your first experiences with Thom Gunn these early poems, and is that why you went to that talk expecting to not be impressed?

AK: Yes.

SC: What was your relationship to the work; how much had you been exposed to him prior to hearing him speak?

AK: The poetry I knew was mostly in that very well-known, widely published joint *Selected Poems* that he did with Ted Hughes. It didn't interest me at all, nor did Hughes, nor does Hughes. But Thom had a sort of awakening in the mid-60s; part of it was LSD, part of it was coming out as a homosexual, which had been a very onerous thing for him to disguise or repress. I think he also at this point was becoming much more sexually active, more promiscuous than he'd [previously] been. He'd been active. I think Mike mentioned that. And the other thing is he had a bout with hepatitis, serious hepatitis. He was gravely ill. And I think he'd been an ambitious man, he'd described himself as a young poet who got a lot of attention. I think at this point, he just said, "Fuck it. I'm just going to write the kind of poems that I feel like."

But also, it was at a time, I think he was in his mid-late 30s. When a poet either blooms or withers, or becomes conventional … It involved great risks, and becoming the poet he did essentially closed the door on his reputation in Britain, although he'd be loath to admit it. I think that hurt him. He got some rough treatment. It would hurt anybody, particularly someone who'd been so lauded, and was then treated as the largest disappointment of his generation; he showed so much promise and went to America, and just became "a loose drug-taking fag writing free verse." So it was a disappointment he became his own man. Another thing was that he was on the tenure track at University California–Berkeley, and it was stifling his writing, and he quit.

SC: I think that's really brave as well, to pass up that to focus on something else.

AK: Tremendous, tremendous. Because he didn't have a financial cushion, but he had a couple of friends in the department there, influential friends. One was Tom Parkinson, and one was Josephine Miles, and they gave him a situation that only one other poet at the time in America had, which is working one semester a year, and that was Richard Wilbur, who by that point had won the Pulitzer and the National Book Award. He was already regarded as a major figure in American poetry. Thom was not.

He kept that situation in place, where he taught for the spring. He worked in that capacity for the next 30 years or so. It was a modest income, but it was enough. He's someone who needed both freedom and containment, otherwise he, I think, he got a little loose and crazy. He was contained for four or five months a year, and it suited him. He'd start getting grumpy in December or so as he began planning for his teaching semester, because he took it very seriously, and continued to be grumpy through much of the semester. He threw himself into it. And when it was over, he just about was running around naked with his dick in his hand.

I remember him walking down Cole Street, I think he was my age, not much younger. He was a magnificent specimen. He was wearing tight leather pants and he was shirtless. I recognized when he was in that "cruise control" mode. And he was headed down to a bar on Haight Street. His chest hair was gray, and I said, "What an outrageous spectacle!" And this is my friend. When he was in that mode, he didn't like to be disturbed, it was like when a dog is eating or something like that. I said, "This is extraordinary!" This shy, rather formal Englishman and he'd proceed in that mode until the next December.

SC: This is one of the things I find really fascinating about him. I think in one of the interviews that I've got with him, he says, "My life insists on continuities between the US and Britain, between the formed and informal, between the finite and the infinite." And I think there's always this astonishing generative tension in his work. And I think you're absolutely right. It becomes far stronger later on, because there's always something repressed in the earlier collections that he allows to sort of flourish after *My Sad Captains* and *Jack Straw's Castle*. Do you see that tension as well? How conscious of those kind of tensions in his work do you think he was? Because what you were saying about Auden, I think you're absolutely right. There's something else artificial. When Auden tries to adopt an American voice, it doesn't really work at all. But Gunn's poetics perhaps assimilate the American aesthetic, or what do you think happened there?

AK: Well I think it's a psychological thing as one gets older as an artist. You learn about what kind of ground you flourish in, and you cultivate that ground, and you learn how to cultivate that ground. And that takes years. A lot of artists I think are in denial about it or just don't figure it out, or don't have the discipline. And also if you have a job and a wife and children, you don't have the luxury of doing those sorts of things. But given his situation, and living where he was living, when he was living here, he was able to discover about himself, what made him thrive both as an artist and as a person, psychologically, sexually. And that's a rare thing.

SC: I think what I found amazing looking at the archives at Berkeley [Gunn's main archive is held at the Bancroft Library] is how meticulous and organized and thorough he was, that I had no sense of, I mean obviously he's very formally astute, but I have no sense of him being this incredibly disciplined person as well, and then that, alongside this real hell-raising streak, just a very unexpected combination in a person. We were talking about his meticulousness in his teaching and his thoroughness, and how he gave it his all. Was that one of the aspects of his life where he surprised you, or did you always know he was incredibly organized and thorough? Was that much clear, from just knowing him?

AK: Yes. When he cooked, he was like that. He would cook out of a cookbook, reading it with his eyeglasses on tip of his nose, and be very stern, and not engage in conversation, not drinking.... It's just part of his character. If we met at Zazie's he was punctual, and if he was late, he'd be very apologetic.

SC: That was his favorite lunch spot?

AK: Yes. That's really where we conducted our social life for the most part. We'd have lunch every few weeks. And after he retired, more often. And we'd have lunch, and then go off to see a movie and have couple of drinks, he liked to do that. I think he liked to do that because he felt that I liked to do that. And he'd get a little frisky when he'd had a couple of drinks. We got very close those last few years because we were spending a lot of time together. And we had wonderful afternoons, they started at noon and we'd get off N-Judah train at four or five and maybe get a drink, and then he'd go off back home. Once he was very apologetic; he had a younger man waiting for him, "I've got to go, so-and-so's waiting for me, we have some porn movies. I'm kind of bored." He was an odd mix of formality and abandon, and lovely.

SC: That's what absolutely fascinates me about him, I think. I wonder if you don't mind talking a little about his death. I think you're absolutely right by the way about him being disgruntled by old age. He writes in one of his diaries, a few weeks before he dies, "I'm doing all this speed with this one particular chap and if I continue to do this, I shall surely die." He had high blood pressure, and it seems like he's very aware of the fact that he's really dicing with the possibility of death. Was that anything he expressed, or do you think that he just thought "I'm going to go hell-bent for leather, until I'm done." Do you think he was just unwilling to curtail his lifestyle or do you think he sort of upped it?

AK: I think he upped it, I think he was ready to go. He was showing alarming symptoms of, I think, having taken too much speed on a regular basis. If I saw him early in the week sometimes, his speech was like that of a stroke victim.

SC: Really?

AK: Mike and his roommates spoke with him about it. I mentioned it to him once; he didn't like it. But I felt obliged; I guess for my own selfish reasons I just said it. But it's quite evident to me that he was leaning on it very hard. You couldn't commit that kind of insult to your body at that age without a dire result. His partners, particularly toward the end, were sort of quasi-criminal characters who, I guess, were helping him to get drugs. At one point one of them had given him some heroin along with speed, and he had a very, very bad reaction. Really scared him. I know it did because he spoke to me about it. He vowed never to do that again, but he did do that again the night he died.

SC: Oh, really?

AK: As I understand it. It might've been a lover encouraging him to do it. And he was a fool for love. But it was a multi-polysubstance abuse, whatever overabundance was on the medical report. So no, I wasn't surprised. He also was having some health problems, I think. He imminently needed some hip surgery. He wasn't as attractive to younger men as he had been although still a strikingly handsome older man. He was seventy-five. He law of diminishing returns kicks in for someone who lived, essentially, for sex.

SC: Absolutely. I wonder if you'd mind if I asked you now about the poems that you've written for Gunn, the poem for his sixtieth birthday "After Catullus" and also your poem "In Memoriam." The poems that you directed toward him, how much were they about his poetry as well?

AK: "After Catullus" didn't really have anything to do with him, but after the fact I thought it was something he'd like and a bit saucy. It was at the time, it was his sixtieth birthday. And he did like it, he loved it. You know, he was very naughty, he loved naughty. The "In Memoriam" thing was very much occasioned by his death, and my missing his presence in the neighborhood, and that particularly touching song "I Thought About You." [AK informs me he was thinking of the Shirley Horn version]. His own poetry wasn't particularly an influence on mine, because we were, we did such different things. But the way he'd thought about poetry, and approached material wasn't a large influence, I don't know how clear that is. We have a poem we wrote on the same subject, with the same title, almost simultaneously, called "Tenderloin." It's just a curiosity and it's interesting, in how he treated essentially the same patch of turf. He was amused. We felt amused when it came to pass....

SC: I'm just thinking, I know what's going to come up on the next contemporary poetry examination I set, a compare and contrast between the two, that would be great. I was very curious about your poetic sequence "The History of Western Music": you've got several poems entitled that, and then "In Memoriam Thom Gunn," how did you have a sense of that fitting into a sequence of on Western music and those type of songs?

AK: Well, because there was a musical component.

SC: Okay.

AK: So I use it very loosely. But also, I suppose, it was a way of tempering or camouflaging an emotionally difficult subject. A way to handle in form really, because it followed the form of a song, but definitely it was a musical structure.

SC: And can I ask you, and you can tell me to mind my own business, but in the poem you say, you keep on thinking of something "you said to me once." And I was curious about what it was, because it's not revealed in the poem, and it stays private and intimate, and if you wish to retain that privacy I do understand, but I'd be very curious to know it was.

AK: I don't think it was anything in particular. I think it was probably something of a self-destructive nature, or something that revealed to me that he was heading to check out. I had a brother who did that. I knew months in advance that he was going to kill himself so I was sensitive to the dynamic. I know Thom, like my brother, was probably not a drama queen. But they were going to do it, one way or another. And there was nothing I could do to stop it.

SC: It is a wonderful poem. I was re-reading it again this morning, and I've got a particular interest in elegy for poets. I think Thom kind of proved quite hard to elegize, but for a start I think there's something different between the "In Memoriam" poem and the elegiac poem, and I know that Clive Wilmer, his friend in Cambridge tried as well, but there really aren't as many elegies done as you'd think there would be. Do you think that's because he's almost impossible to contain, because that's one of the things that I'm endlessly fascinated about him.

He starts out in Cambridge being taught by F. R. Leavis, emulating the Elizabethan poets, writing in meter and rhyme. Comes to America, studies with Yvor Winters, is in San Francisco at the time of the Beat poets, but is not *of* the Beat poets. Writes poems about the AIDS epidemic from the frontlines but at the same time manages to be very objective about that. He's always moving on from what he called "categorizing foolishness," and do you think the fact that you can't categorize him, that he continually evades and eludes, that's one of the reason he hasn't been elegized. I think the best commemorations are those in the *Threepenny Review* where other people reminisce about him, just as you are now. He seems far better suited to reminiscence rather than formal poetic memorialization. Do you think that speaks as a function of the person he was?

AK: Yeah, in part, and it's part of the poet he was. Among other reasons, Thom was a wonderful elegiac poet. So don't try to con a con man. Don't try to elegize an elegiac poet.

SC: I think that's a very acute observation, and actually my PhD was on elegies on poets, and there were very few elegies for elegists. It becomes almost impossible to do so. I don't think anyone attempted it with Milton, for example, I think that's absolutely right. And what do you think of Gunn's critical reception? For example, there's this collection of essays edited by Joshua Weiner that's coming out with the University of Chicago Press. Do you think he's going to increasingly be assimilated in a way that he perhaps wasn't in his lifetime? I mean, it came to my attention after *The Man with Night Sweats*, which is I think when he saw a resurgence in Britain. What do you think his poetic legacy is likely to be? Do you think he's going to be canonized, would you think that sort of outside rebel persona will be incorporated into the edifice of letters?

AK: Yes, I mean if anyone's reading in 20 years. It's a very complicated proposition. He's difficult to categorize as someone like Heaney or Hughes is not. They fit very neatly into a "serious poet" category, and in their relationship with the English and Irish traditions, Anglo-Irish tradition. I hope that over time people will see the scale of [Gunn's] achievement. I was really impressed by it when I was doing *Gunn's Selected Poems*.... I really have thought all along that people have him all wrong, they admire him for the wrong reasons, they disapprove of him for the wrong reasons. They just don't get it.

And he's also an uneven poet, because he tried different things. He was not content to stay in the same place or write the same poem. So I'm hoping the *Selected* that FSG and Faber did, and the larger selected poems that Clive Wilmer's working on [this was published in

2017], will raise his work to greater prominence. And also down the road his letters, so they'll see what an extraordinary, brilliant, wild, unusual, extreme, and decent character he was. The letters he wrote to Douglas Chambers, which are at the University of Toronto, are wonderfully entertaining. I think that Clive is getting together some letters, by Tony Tanner and others, that will be fantastic.

SC: And what would you think would be a good way of approaching Thom as the subject of a Biography? I actually found in his notebooks, something that he entitled "Plan For My Autobiography" and it's incredibly thoroughly delineated, and he even lists photographs that he'd like to include. And my feeling is that as much as possible, I'd like to follow Thom's own plan if I were his biographer. How would you approach this particular task? Because I'd also be very keen to place the onus on his poetry, but then again you're falling into a trap, because he's always changing what he's doing. Even though he's associated with something such as the Beats or Winters, he's not actually adhering to that and, anyhow, that becomes very limiting. So I'm probably putting you on the spot, but how would you approach a task like this?

AK: I think for any biographer addressing any subject, the trick is to find a way in to both the character and the work with an approach that feels comfortable and right: what needs to get said and how it best gets said. The biographer's relationship with the subject is paramount.

SC: I think the problem that he's always posed to whoever writes about him, or whoever edits him—and I'm sure you found this with the *Selected*—is how to describe the arc of his career without it being disjoined, for, as you said, he's very inconsistent. How did you get round that with the *Selected*? Did you agonize over any of the selections—in particular, for example, the early collections? Were you not so keen to include those, or did you feel that was essential to understanding how he got to where he got, to have the early foundations?

AK: I would have been content not to have included anything from the early collections, but Paul Keegan at Faber recommended that

I include some. I think I maybe added just a couple of poems, and Paul suggested that I have more, which is probably a good idea, otherwise it would have seemed too idiosyncratic. And again, in Britain particularly, his reputation rests. Even some of the reviewers of the *Selected* people were rather perplexed and mildly appalled that I picked so parsimoniously from the early work. But no, I didn't struggle. It was a wonderful experience really, because it got me much closer to the work. And I learned a lot and, again, became a good deal more appreciative. I thought there was quite a bit in the *oeuvre* that fails, which other people could find very important among the poems. But when I got done with it, I thought to myself, "This is a hell of a book." You know, he's a great poet!

SC: Could I ask you just one last question: I do realize I've been talking your ear off for an hour now.... You described him as an Elizabethan poet, and I know that one of the essays in the Weiner collection looks at that and his relationship to Elizabethans. How would you describe that briefly? I mean, do you mean he's a metaphysical poet, or he's got these highly wrought forms that he's using to discuss very colloquial and quotidian matters? What do you exactly mean by Elizabethan?

AK: Well, the formal containment of very personal, emotional material certainly, but also the anonymous voice of the Elizabethan.

SC: Right.

AK: The absence of personality.

SC: Well, thank you very much for taking the time to talk to me.

AK: Lovely to talk to you, madam.

SC: Thank you. I'll stop torturing you with this device now.

2. In Conversation with Karl Miller

SC: I wonder if you can tell me about your meeting Thom at Cambridge and about your years together there.

KM: Yes. I can do that. There's quite a lot of stuff to tell, of course, because I knew him for some few years. He and I read English under Leavis. I was under Leavis and he was a sanitary distance from Leavis in Trinity College, but he was interested in Leavis; and we had a friend in Tony White who was also at Downing, studying with Leavis as I was.

So that's how we came together. And we did a number of things together, publishing, for example, anthologies. Thom did one called *Poetry from Cambridge,* and I contributed to that, and then he contributed to one that I did called *Poetry from Cambridge Subsequently.* And there are a lot of good poets in there; not just Thom, Ted Hughes as well. It's a kind of small, blue book, the one I did, which is now hard to get hold of, even costly I think. But in its own way, as far as a history of post-war English poetry goes, it has a certain place. There were quite a few good poets there.

And I helped to publish a magazine called *Granta,* which we wrote for, and Ted, and we were very thick and friendly with one another all through that period. And then after Cambridge he went to America. And I only saw him after that quite briefly. I saw him in America. In my memory it was San Antonio, we went swimming—

SC: He did teach in San Antonio for a short time.

KM: Yes. Well, that's what I remember, a swimming expedition to a pool. And we've got pictures of that. And I also, I think, saw him in a house of his in Stanford or Berkeley or something. That must have been on a different occasion. I went two or three times to America for the *New Statesman* as a journalist. I also went round America as a Commonwealth Fellow when I was at Harvard. So one of the calls could have been made as a Commonwealth Fellow.

So I saw a lot of him. And then he took up with Mike Kitay and settled in America. And we drifted apart. Quite why we did is not clear to me to this day, because I don't think I did anything to outrage him, and he did nothing to outrage me. But I think he lost interest in England. And I was a specimen of England. And that may have come into it.

Equally, he had become openly gay by then. He told me he was gay at Cambridge when we were students together. And this was a big deal, of course, a momentous statement he was making, and I think he may have thought I would have disapproved of it, and this may have added a certain tension to our relationship which was then compounded by his becoming Mike's partner. I never knew Mike very well but I had no hostility to him at all, and none to his being gay. I suppose I must have assumed, or must have been very stupid, if I didn't assume that he was interested in the homosexual life before his telling me as much. And of course he was one of several gay people whom I was friendly with and he was friendly with. He wasn't the only black sheep; there was a flock!

There was somehow the idea that I was somehow placed in relation to these developments in a way that meant that we could no longer be friends, given of course that he was in America. And I didn't see him very often, and he didn't come back very often. He kept up with Tony White, as I understand. But I didn't see much of him in this country, not from the point of his Mayflowering out to America. Once he got on that boat, he stayed there.

SC: Did he talk about his decision to go to Stanford and study with Winters with you?

KM: Oh, we discussed that, yes. Winters' work was known to both of us. And we both expected him to be Leavisian in style, a severe American Puritan. But he was rather refreshing and a powerful presence for us in those days. And he wrote some good books, which I duly studied; it was dreadfully unintelligible to me, a fact that was probably quite a good thing. And Thom set himself to study with Winters. The point I'm not doing justice to is that my connection to him is very strongly grounded in my interest in his developing poetry, his developing gift for poetry. Because it was apparent to me right from the start, as was Hughes, that these were very good poets, and it was exciting to me. More than exciting, inspiring to be in a position to talk to Thom about his poetry and other people's poetry. So that's what gave the substance to our friendship as much as anything. It wasn't all serious. We had a laugh.

In the case of Ted, there was much less intimacy. Not that I had anything against Ted, I liked him. I liked his writing, too. But it just didn't work out that I knew him the same way. Thom and I, for example, had a connection with what was known as the English Club at Cambridge. Used to invite wiseacres down to talk to us and that kind of thing. We helped to run that. I think he probably was the president before I was, or something. Maybe he was a year ahead of me at Cambridge. I'm not absolutely sure about that.

SC: I think he was.

KM: Yes.

SC: He was born in 1929, and then he did two years' National Service.

KM: Right, so did I. I was born in '31, however. So he was ahead of me. He wasn't two years ahead of me. I think he was one year. Could be wrong about that. But it was as if he was in the same year. We went to the same lectures and so on.

SC: So your interest in him initially was poetic.

KM: Well, I mean, it wasn't poetic in the sense that I wasn't indifferent to the sort of person he was and I enjoyed his company. We had a lot in common. But the poetry, of course, as I said, gave substance to the friendship. More substance perhaps than it might have if he had only been interested in lacrosse or something. He wasn't interested in football or sport; I was. So I struggled onto the football pitch for something like 10 years after Cambridge. We were none of us all that great at football, but we were very keen. I still am. He wasn't keen.

SC: No, I've found no reference to it in any of his papers.

KM: I don't think so.

SC: What do you remember of the critical reception of *Fighting Terms*? It was quite a literary sensation at the time.

KM: It started off very promisingly, yes. Well, I wasn't surprised that it took, because I already thought well of it and wrote a profile of him at that time in the university magazine.

SC: Is that the one where you described his "ear-splitting laugh"?

KM: Yes. That one. And that was, I think, acknowledging that he was a good writer and ought to be treated as such. That was the idea. Yeah, he was very much a force, and certainly a force in my life. What else is there about the Cambridge scene which, some of this will become apparent in my piece in the *Raritan Review*. Because there's just that amount of detailed quotation material which might be of interest to you. I think I've covered the salient points, though, as far as that's concerned.

But you asked me about how it happened: he was taken up as a British poet, a young newcomer who was likely to do well. Well, I was pleased by that. He was associated, as you know, with the Movement. And the Movement, in a crocodilian way, snapped him up. They wanted him to be in the Movement. And he didn't have any very deep natural affinity with the Movement is the truth. But he had no objection to being taken seriously by the Movement. He was sometimes anthologized with them, that kind of thing. But his status as a Movementeer is not certain. And I don't think he wanted to be thought of for the rest of his life as a Movement poet.

SC: I think the further he got away from it, the less he wanted to be affiliated with it.

KM: Yes, that's right. It began to seem like England, you see. That was the point. It began to seem like England's defense. And of course they made a great song and dance about being English and somehow standing for England while also, of course, pissing on England, complaining about English life, but nonetheless there was some essential Larkinian phonic essence there, which they voted for. There's a new book called *The Movement*, edited by Zachary Leader. I've got a piece in there which mentions Gunn quite a bit. So I was pleased about that and felt—but then he was gone. He was gone to America. Like one of those cowboys in the poem by Donald Davie, out west, he went out west. So I didn't see him as much anymore for reasons I've given you. I don't think it would be right to say that I was bringing any problematic attitudes to the question of being gay. I mean, almost half the men I know are gay. I find it easier to understand men who like women. But that's not at all to say that I don't sympathize with the other thing. And I certainly don't have any objection to people finding love with members of their own sex.

SC: It's interesting that you mention Donald Davie, because I know that he and Gunn had quite a fractious relationship because of Davie's very, very uncomfortable stance on homosexuality.

KM: That's right. Davie was a prig, as you probably gathered. And although he always spoke very respectfully of Thom, I was a little surprised by that, because I thought he would have found out that Thom was on drugs or gay or some damn thing, and that he wouldn't have been able to take that. Well, I got some inkling of his objections to that, but he'd gone on better with him and respected him as a writer throughout it. Nonetheless, I'm sure Thom must have thought that Davie was a Puritan and a prig. How could he not? He was.

SC: Davie pronounced that no good literature had ever come of homosexuality or something extraordinary.

KM: Not that I know of, but it's quite possible.

SC: And so it's very interesting that you say that Gunn told you at Cambridge that he was gay, because I didn't— 'cause I've been trying to figure out when he actually did come out to his friends.

KM: Well that would have been, I'm bad on dates, I can't remember the year I left Cambridge. What year did he leave Cambridge?

SC: I think it must have been '52, '53? Is it? Or have I got that completely wrong? [He graduated in 1952].

KM: As late as that? I'm not sure. But it was just before he left that he told me, something I more or less must have known. But you know, it—as I was saying, there were lots of you in the same boat. And then when I went to Harvard, I was plying my way through Harvard University, before discovering half the people I knew there were homosexual. Half, at least! The whole geography department was closed down because of the incidence of gay teachers at one point, I'm told.

SC: Really?

KM: So I'm told. That was before my time. But all my friends at Bard College were homosexual. One of my greatest friends anywhere was flamboyantly homosexual. A man called Marius Bewley who taught at Rutgers university, was a friend of Leavis's, concealing his sexual orientation for a while, or trying to, or not trying very hard to, because Leavis didn't seem to have it quite sorted out in his mind. They were very slow-witted about things like that sometimes, even Leavis, in those days. But Donald had been in the world, he would have known the score. He didn't like the score in some respects, but also I think liking Thom.

SC: I found a series of very tetchy letters between the two.

KM: Oh, really?

SC: It's all about, Gunn being—

KM: Well Donald didn't mind writing letters straight from the shoulder about this and that. We fell out about politics eventually. Donald got involved at Essex University with student unrest in the '60s. And the faculty divided. Donald was disliked by some of the students and some of the faculty. And he hated students protesting, too much so, in my view. I didn't much like the protesting students of the '60s, but some of it makes sense, it seemed to me, and so I certainly couldn't say the things he used to say. I think things got a bit sourer in life in general for Donald. He went back to America, I believe to another professorial Chair after that, after the row. But I'm not too well-briefed on that.

The position that I tried to defend in that *Raritan* article I don't think is acceptable to various Gunnians at my elbow in London, like Peter Swaab, who's devoted to Gunn. I did show him the piece, and he didn't raise any objection, though he can't have liked it. Because what I was saying, I was interested in approaching Thom's poetry from the point of view of his rising to occasions, a response to something public, something in the social background or social history that he inhabited, which in my view produced very good results on two separate occasions.

First of all, in the '60s when he "became" gay and sided with toughies and all that, and motorbikes and so on, "On the Move," across the globe, all that, you may not go along with all the articles in the faith at that point, but I think it was good for his poetry. I think he wrote well about these things. It excited him, and he responded. That is what I was pursuing in this article. And I said that produced some of his best poetry, and so did the outbreak of AIDS at the other end of his life—

SC: Absolutely.

KM: Where there was a challenge not totally different. I mean, different in the sense that it was a grim, bleak challenge, whereas the other one was ostensibly useful and optimistic at the beginning of his life. At the end of his life, of course there was the fact of death and people dying, his friends dying, and that must have marked him because he'd gotten into a way of life which proclaimed itself as joyous and liberated. He'd always liked going to bed with people that were having a good time.

Well, a lot of the people he left behind in England were struggling when it came to having a good time of that sort. They weren't doing all these amusing things that he was doing, and then joy was on his banner. But then of course as gods usually provide, there was a revenge, wasn't there? And the illness spread, and these poor people had to face their deaths. So it was a joy that reached a bitter end, you could say. And I don't know what his end was like, though I've been told with people like James Campbell that the problem to do with drug-taking got worse. Did you know him?

SC: I didn't know Gunn, but I've read through all of the diaries from those years, and he was very frank about his drug use, but he was taking a lot of speed, and he was a man of 72, 73 taking speed, and he had high blood pressure, so I think that's what did for him, really. But several people have said to me, among them August Kleinzahler, that they think he quite deliberately knew what he was doing. That he didn't envisage this as a way of having a long life, it was just he would rather—

KM: Well, he was suicidal that way.

SC: Well, it was self-destructive, but he got very sick of being old. He'd been a very handsome man, and now he couldn't attract people in the same way, and that that way of life—

KM: Ah, to hell with him. What did he expect at 75? For God's sake! But still of course you're right about that, that would have been a factor. On the other hand, when I last saw him, he must have been 70 or thereabouts, and he was looking like he was up for it then. He was quite handsome-looking and dyed his hair heavily. He had black hair, rather than white hair, and he made some reference to going to a room where his old former friends were gathered, and they were all wearing snow on their heads. He thought that was very droll. Meanwhile he, I think, was not wearing snow on his head. He was wearing black lacquer.

SC: I didn't realize that he dyed his hair.

KM: Well, I'm not sure about that, but he did have black hair, didn't he?

SC: I think he definitely got very salt-and-pepper later on.

KM: Yes, he certainly—that would have been a phase too. But that doesn't matter, it's just that when I saw him, he seemed to me to be the sort of person who would still want to attract people and have love affairs. But I know nothing about it more than that.

SC: Can I ask you about his "Mayflowering," because one of the aspects that really interests me is the condition of being an Anglo-American poet. Do you think that the sort of British literary establishment took against him in the '60s because he'd become the symbol of a son of Albion who's gone abroad and completely sloughed off this English poetic?

KM: "He betrayed his country!" Well, it's a complicated answer needed for that, because the fact is, there would have been some resentment of him. But that was probably outweighed by the opposite. There was some sense that this was ironically glamorous. It was like going to Missolonghi like Byron, going to a romantic place and living a liberated life. So it was even a trace of envy, so it was a mixed picture, I think. No, all the people I knew were friendly with him and had no hostility to him for being in America. And there would have been a few mincing literati in London maybe who would formulate an objection, but I don't think it was very prominent. He became pretty well regarded in England. More so than in America.

SC: Yeah, I think that that's interesting as well, the way in which he was viewed in the different countries.

KM: He was more successful for more time here than there. I've never fully understood why that's so. But after all, Larkin was quite unsuccessful in America until very late on in his living and posthumous career. They was a period when they didn't know who he was in America, for example, in the '60s.

SC: And I completely agree with what you've said about him being an occasional poet in so much as he rises to occasions. Even one of his essay collections was called *The Occasions of Poetry*, and I think the way he applies form to these experiences of the infinite, for example in *Moly*, or the way that he uses form to contain the unthinkable when he's writing about the AIDS epidemic are some of the things that interest me most about him. Which would you say were his strongest collections? Would you say *The Man with Night Sweats* and *Moly*?

KM: Yes, and the first collection. The first collection was *Fighting Terms*, wasn't it?

SC: Yeah, and then *The Sense of Movement* was the Winters-inflected one.

KM: Yes, *The Sense of Movement*. I like both of those collections. *Moly* I like, and *The Man with Night Sweats*. Mid-period Gunn, after he'd been exposed to Winters, had a certain "prize poem" aspect to it. And some of the poems seem to me to lack fire or feeling. They were too clever, you know, and that kind of thing, in the mid-period, some poems seem to me. I didn't understand some of them. I have to check about which of them. Well I'm a great one for complaining about not understanding poets. I think that poems in the *TLS*, for example, 90% are unintelligible. I really do think that. I could easily prove it by asking the people who wrote them what they mean. Of course, you don't always have to know what a poem means, do you?

SC: I think it's very liberating to be able to admit that you don't understand it. Because I think half the time it is the emperor's new clothes.

KM: Oh, absolutely so.

SC: Everybody's far too terrified to admit!

KM: And emperor's new clothes is one of the fine myths of literary deception, I think. Absolutely. Well, I tried to get a woman friend of mine who writes poems published; she's a psychoanalyst who took to writing poems when she was about 50 or 60, and I think they're very good. I can't get any of these people to take notice because they're intelligible, they can be followed!

SC: They're not sufficiently oblique?

KM: Not at all oblique. No, they're not grossly self-apparent, but you can follow what she said. And she's actually rather good.

SC: She's just not very fashionable.

KM: And I'm so angry about it these days. And just had a run-in with one particular editor. And I gave him a very good poem by her which she had shown me. And he reams me out and tells me how it's too long and it's in five verses. You'd think he was suggesting that she remove some of the verses. So I was an editor for donkeys' years—I would never have thought about telling a poet to take some stanzas out![1]

SC: That is amazing.

KM: It is to me amazing. Anyway, in the case of Thom, I think the middle period does contain poems that are too deep for me and take me out of my depth. And some of the simple poems in *The Night Sweats* volume and elsewhere, certainly, are perfectly easy to understand and rather feeling-full poems that make you care about the person including the poet, and the other people who figure in the poems too. I like that.

SC: What did you make of his last collection, *Boss Cupid*, because I was talking with Clive Wilmer at Cambridge last weekend, and—

KM: A great enthusiast of Gunn's!

SC: Yes, absolutely. And he was saying that he felt very much as if Gunn knew that this was his last collection. That it has this sort of structure to it that suggests that it's a capstone collection. It begins with an *ars poetica* in the poem "Duncan" and finishes with a sort of final bow. And it's also the first collection in which he really writes about his mother and the gas poker.

KM: Yeah, I remember Wilmer's writing about that, it would be in the *TLS*?

SC: Yes.

KM: Well it seemed to me Clive liked it, that he was right about that. The mother thing is very important. I don't think even your disdain for biography will be able to refuse to confront the Minosian image of his mum.

SC: It's when he starts writing, his first diary in the archive at Berkeley begins the day that he and Ander found his mum dead. And his diary begins, "We found Mother dead today." And I think that's it's the

---

1. Miller was the founding editor of the *London Review of Books*.

absolutely overarching influence in his entire life, and probably the reason that he became a poet.[2]

KM: Well, it was a shaking experience for him that affected him for the rest of his life.

SC: Did he ever speak to you about it?

KM: I didn't often speak to him about it. I did meet her, though. And his father. They had a kind of grace-and-favor newspaper-editor's Mayfair flat. Thom took his sort of shaggy friends round there. And I think she was there on one occasion and so was his father, who was a very rather forbidding, white-haired, grim character. Quite hard to relate to. His mother had very pretty legs in shimmering silk stockings, which I'm afraid I remember!

SC: I'm just wondering, it must be his stepmother, because his mother committed suicide when he was 15.

KM: Well obviously then it must have been his stepmother. She was quite young. So it probably was a step-mother.

SC: Who was much loathed.

KM: Thank you for putting me right about that.

SC: No, not at all.

KM: I was obviously wrong about the year his mother died. I just didn't know enough about it at the time, because I didn't discuss it with him. Clearly it was the man's first wife who killed herself. And then when I saw these people, this was his stepmother, who you tell me he disliked?

SC: Yes. She was much disliked by both Ander who went to live with her, and Thom who disliked her so much that he actually went to live with one of his mother's friends.

---

2. I had the extraordinary experience of discovering his mother's suicide note folded into the leaves of one of Gunn's scrapbooks held at the Bancroft Library at Berkeley. So restrained and understated was the scribbled note that it had been previously overlooked.

KM: In Kent, somewhere?

SC: Those were his aunts, in Snodland in Kent.

KM: Snodland, yes.

SC: And then he lived with his mother's friend Theresa in Hampstead during the term time, when he was at University College School.

KM: I remember getting letters from Snodland. Rather melancholy letters.

SC: Really?

KM: Yes, well, he was lonely.

SC: I think his aunts were quite formidable.

KM: I don't know about them. I never met them. The father was completely impassive. He wouldn't give anything. But then obviously he'd married some beauty from the world of journalism or something, and that's where the silk stockings came from.

SC: Right. His father's name was Herbert Gunn. What was he like?

KM: I'm just telling you, he was impassive and forbidding!

SC: I'm really curious because when I was speaking to Ander Gunn the other day, and he said that he always suspected that his father knew that Thom was gay, and that that was the major rift in their relationship that nothing could ever heal.

KM: No, it's quite likely, I think. He looked as if he would be like that when you met him. Because I didn't actually ask him questions, what he thought of gays!

SC: "So, Mr. Gunn!"

KM: Yeah, that's right, yes. "How are things with your son's latent homosexuality?" No I think that was fair, but I would expect almost certainly there would be ... Can't think what his second wife was doing there. Maybe they were just living in the flat where Thom was. It wouldn't have been very characteristic of Thom to take his undesirable male friends from Cambridge round there. I don't know why he did that. Maybe it was just convenient. We were all in London.

SC: And so when was the last time you saw Thom?

KM: Well, I think the last time was when he gave a reading at Faber and Faber. He got some medal or something from Faber. And he came and read half a dozen poems and spoke about them. That wasn't uplifting for me because he didn't seem to know who I was.

SC: Really?

KM: No. Or my wife.

SC: That's very curious....

KM: There were a lot of people mobbing around him. And I got the impression of a person who was under the influence of drugs. That could be wrong....Perhaps he was just confused by the confusion of the occasion. I'd been waiting for him.

SC: Was that 2002?

KM: I guess it would have been around then, yes. That's the last time. But I had some letters which I exchanged with him on one or two occasions in recent times. Which were rather good letters, I thought, and were friendly. I wrote a memoir called *Rebecca's Vest,* which deals with Thom a bit. And he read it and he was nice about it. He used to think I was a kind of gnarled, unreadable Leavisite when I wrote criticism at Cambridge and he was right about that. I wrote some awful stuff when I was an undergraduate. Not entirely, but most of it. So he was right about that. So I don't suppose he ever developed much of a taste for reading what I wrote.

On the other hand he was perceptive and understanding about my memoir book, which dealt with my early days and stopped after I went to London to work. I don't think it had anything about America much in it. I went for a year or two, as I told you, to Harvard. Greater than two years? Can't have been. Must only just have been the one. But I went right round America with friends, and with my wife, and we got married in America. And the book probably dealt with that, briefly. It dealt with going to Cambridge, I think. And the magazine stuff and the stuff about Thom in it. Stuff you would probably not be surprised by, you would know already, but you could look at it sometime if you want to.

SC: I'll be sure to.

KM: And it talks a bit about blossoming as a poet. That was the main concern expressed there. And as I say, he wrote a very interesting letter about that, which is probably in Emory University [where Karl Miller's papers are held], but I don't think I kept that back, because I had a lot of letters of mine, and as someone at death's door I didn't want to be saddling some poor loved one with piles and piles of letters. So I sifted all the ones by writers and celebrities, because that's what Emory wanted; they wrote to me, you see. And they took them, so that seemed to be a quite reasonable thing to do.

SC: No, absolutely. And I think it's a very difficult for people to know what to do with collections like that. I wonder if I could ask you the question I asked you when we were at lunch, which is, one of the problems I foresee, which is the problem for any biographer, is treading that line between the work and the life, and making sure that the life doesn't overpower the work— What would you recommend?

KM: Yes, yes, that's right, I remember what you said. Well, I have to tell you that I'm of a very firm mind on this subject. I think that if you're writing the life of a writer, you should bring in his personal life a good deal. And you should bring in his writing. And to miss one or the other out, seems to me grotesque. There are people writing biographies now who just don't mention the writer's writings.

SC: Yes. I thought the Hamilton life of Robert Lowell was pretty flawed because of that.

KM: Not enough about the writings.

SC: Yeah.

KM: Well, I think there could have been more about the writings. I think that it should be about both. I think that writings come from the writer. They don't come from anywhere else. If the writer didn't exist, there would be no writings. And what's in the writings is his life! That doesn't mean that Jim in the novel is the same as Jim in the guy's life. It's not going to be like that. You have to exercise a great deal of tact in ascribing the writings to the life. I do understand that. I understand what the snags are.

But I think in the case of Thom, it would be a much better book, from your point of view and from the reader's point of view, if you managed to give a sense of what his life was like and how it relates to the poetry. Clearly the poetry will have in it stuff not perceptible in the life, and the other way round. There'll be stuff in the life that doesn't get in the poetry. But that can all be accommodated by the kind of book I'm talking about. And it makes for a more interesting read, too, if you have some sense of what kind of life produced this set of poems. That seems to me to be the case. For example, the later poems, which deal with AIDS, the cost of AIDs in a circle of friends who really require to be described, and he wrote in a book that you might be writing. Unless it was a completely austere treatise about the poetry; some academic thing that eschewed all personality.

SC: Which I'm not keen to do. I think the life is—

KM: No, there's no point in it. The life is informative.

SC: I suppose what I'm very wary of doing is sensationalizing—I think it would be easy with all the sex and drugs and rock 'n' roll—that it might be quite easy for the poetry to suffer some sort of diminution, if that's what you make it all about, and I think the issue is managing to walk that line. But I don't want to psychopathologize the poems, in the way Plath is often dissected. Her poems are reduced to a symptom of her psychological makeup.

KM: Pathology. They're made into a pathology of her life, you mean.

SC: Yes, which I'm very wary of.

KM: Well, except she was off her head and wrote about it. And her poems relate to this. But I quite agree that to bring forward mostly some fancy psychogenic explanation of why her poems are as they are is a mistake. Apart from anything else, most of the books I've read on Plath, and I seem to have read not all, only about thirty thousand, seems to tend very much to the airing of theories about her mentality and so on, don't they? And the mythology and all the rest of it. That doesn't mean that you can't treat these things but that to build a psychological system which lends explanations for what Plath did seems pointless to me and they're usually wrong. And I've had the experience of talking to Ted Hughes' sister-in-law about her interpretation of Sylvia's poems and whatever you said was in the poem, she disagreed. And possibly, she was right.

SC: Is this Olwyn?

KM: Olwyn, yes. You run into her?

SC: No, I never have.

KM: She's quite a formidable character.

SC: I imagine so. I've spoken to people who've tried to get permissions to quote from Hughes' poems....

KM: Well, Olwyn's quite a clever woman, but very strange. And possessive. And doesn't like Plath.

SC: At all. No, I don't think there was much love lost between them in life as well....

KM: Oh, no, not at all.

SC: There's some quite spiteful letters from Plath about Olwyn to her [Plath's] mother.

KM: I certainly sided with Plath on that. I mean Olwyn could be a bit nightmarish. Ted, fortunately, was an easy kind of chap.

You know, I wouldn't hesitate to write about what kind of person Thom was. You didn't know him, so you were in a way both helped and hindered by not knowing him. In a way it's better that you didn't know him. Because there are books to be written by people who did know him, who'd be able to give some vivid account of what sort of person he was. Which I haven't really provided you with, even though I knew him quite well, and in the beginning was solid with him in his adventures into poetry. Which made a lot of sense to me. I wish I could have done what he did, and write as he did. So I was envious of it, but I don't think I had bad feelings about him being a success. Bad feelings come very easily to writers as you know. About each other. But in that respect, I don't think I ever have had bad feelings.

The end, you describe very well how he was at the end of the day. Aging, losing the comforts of having a healthy life, and then the wrestling with drugs and taking risks with his heart and his blood pressure. I mean the story I was told initially may have been inaccurate, that he was really unable to shed the heroin addiction, and was holed up in his room, not coming out.

SC: I never heard of a heroin addiction. I'd heard that he'd taken LSD and crystal meth, but I never heard anything—

KM: Well, that might be wrong, so don't take it as right.

SC: No, it's very interesting.

KM: I don't know, it might be quite wrong. I know nothing about drugs, and so I'm only going on the word that was dropped by somebody who claimed to know something about it. But he could have been wrong.

SC: My understanding is that he'd go on speed benders, and then stay awake for days and days at a time and then crash. But there's an entry in his diary maybe two and a half, three weeks before he dies, and it says, "If I go on like this, I shall surely die." And so I think he did know what he was doing, I think he just got fed up and decided to go out with a bang rather than a whimper.

KM: Well, was it a bang?

SC: I don't know, I suppose, if you spent most of your adult life cruising gay bars and finding men, to do that on the last night of your life, maybe that is the way you'd want to go.

KM: He did that, didn't he? He brought somebody back and then that person found himself with a dead man.

SC: Yep. And then he fled.

KM: And had to make his getaway. Yes, I heard that. Yes, that doesn't mean he was either committing suicide or not committing suicide, though. He was overtaken by possibly a heart attack, wasn't he?

SC: Yes.

KM: If he had blood pressure problems, he could have gone through a heart attack any time, I suppose.

SC: Well thank you very much indeed for taking the time to talk to me. I greatly appreciate it.

KM: Not at all.

IV.
Au Contraire:
The Condition
of the Irish-English

The Irish-English

Interviewer: *"Vous êtes Anglais Monsieur Beckett?"*
Samuel Beckett: *"Au contraire."*

I've always loved Samuel Beckett's definition of Irishness as being contrary to Englishness but I'm also at odds with it. This is because I am both Irish and English and, consequently, more conflicted than contrary. I also have the added complication of expatriation since I moved to America in 2004.

I should clarify early on exactly what I mean by my coinage "Irish-English." Of course, the usual formulation is Anglo-Irish but I wish to indicate something other. In particular, I chose to use "English" rather than "Anglo" to connote a linguistic heritage rather than religious affiliation. Prior to the time of Irish independence the Anglo-Irish were a distinct ruling class in Ireland that were brought in to govern after the Protestant Ascendancy into the seventeenth century. They governed until the founding of the Irish Free State in 1922. Under their rule using the Irish Gaelic language was strongly discouraged and pushed right to the remotest fringes of the island (the "Gaeltacht") while the practice of Catholicism was forbidden under the Penal Laws. Anglo-Irish literature has typically been defined as those works written in the English language produced by members of that Protestant ruling elite during that period, including, for example, Maria Edgeworth, William Carelton, Jonathan Swift, Oliver Goldsmith, Richard Sheridan, Bram Stoker and Oscar Wilde. My use of the term Irish-English, though, refers to those who primarily identify with the Irish part of their hybrid and hyphenated selves after the founding of the Irish Free State in 1922. I use "English" throughout this essay in the sense far more of the language than the place (after all, England is but one of the four countries that make up the United Kingdom of Great Britain and Northern Ireland).

Let us consider the Irish identities of the first three of the four Irish winners of the Nobel Prize for Literature after the award's inception in 1901 (the Prize was suspended for the duration of both

World Wars): W. B. Yeats in 1923 (born in Dublin 1865, died on the French Riviera 1939); George Bernard Shaw in 1925 (born in Dublin 1856, died in Hertfordshire, England 1950); and Samuel Beckett in 1969 (born in Dublin 1906, died in Paris 1989). Anglo-Irish all, all born into various flavors of Protestant families of varying degrees of illustriousness, all were born in the Irish capital and died away from their native land, having expatriated themselves from Ireland. Compare the trajectory of these writers' careers to that of the most recent Irish Nobel Laureate, Seamus Heaney, who was awarded the prize in 1995. Heaney is the only one of these winners to have been born outside of the Irish Republic. He was born to a Catholic family 1939 in British-controlled Derry in Northern Ireland and was educated there at Queens University (named after the British monarch of course). Yet, he is the only one of these individuals who became Irish by choice rather than birth, surrendering his blue British passport up and taking Irish citizenship on moving south of the border in 1972. Most interestingly for my expatriated purposes, he spent much of the latter part of his career in America, returning to Ireland from 2006 until his death in the summer of 2013. Though Heaney would always identify himself as Irish he is the perfect example of what I would consider to be an Irish-English poet.

* * *

So am I Anglo-Irish or Irish-English? The latter, I'd say. I have an Irish last name and one of my distant relatives according to family lore, James Connolly, was among the "certain men / the English shot" that W. B. Yeats wrote of in "Easter 1916." I hold an Irish passport, and, I am told, look about as Irish as it's possible to. Certainly the genetic test I took out a fit of curiosity bears that out: my phenotype is entirely Celtic, mostly Irish, a bit Scottish and Breton with a smidge of Iberian thrown in for good measure. My black hair and green eyes certainly fit with the myth of the "Black Irish": those Irish descended from Spanish Armada sailors shipwrecked on the wild western coast of Ireland in the sixteenth century. I was, however, born in the United Kingdom just north of London to an Irish Catholic father and a Protestant English mother of mostly Scottish descent. Their families were horrified by the union and it was only when my mother informed her parents that she was going to run off with her Italian musician boyfriend to entertain at the court of the Shah of Iran that my British grandmother relented and decided my Irish father was the lesser of the two possible evils. Their marriage in 1970 did little, however, to heal the family schism; "I simply can't understand how any rational and sane person could not be a Catholic," my Irish grandmother would helpfully opine to my nominally Anglican mother. Putting aside the rationality of Marian dogmas and the finer points of transubstantiation, her position, was, perhaps, understandable given the fact that she came from a proudly Fenian Wexford family and her brother, Tommy Kielty, had fought for the Irish Republican Army against the English during the Irish Civil War. The English then repaid him by interning him in the remotest Scottish Highlands.

My birth in 1976 precipitated a full-scale family crisis. Into which faith was I to be baptized? My parents, by that point disabused of any affinity with organized religion after a stint as hippies on an Israeli kibbutz, suggested that if I had to be christened it should be at whichever religious establishment was closest to St. Albans City Hospital. My grandmother, fueled with the sort of zeal one can only muster when saving someone's immortal soul, paced out the distances to all nearby places of worship. She triumphed by discovering that the Maryland Rest Home on an obscure unpaved road near the hospital was also, technically, a Catholic convent. Her victory, though, was short-lived. I remain a heathen. She died just before I was due to get dunked.

Would I feel more Irish if Granny had prevailed and I'd been a Catholic? Along with my Irish passport I also hold a British one that asserts that I am protected by the formidable powers of "her Britainnic Majesty." I attended school and university in the United Kingdom and speak with a clipped English accent. That accent would, however, mellow into a brogue over the long happy summers I spent in Ireland with my grandparents at the family home, Sweetmount. When in Ireland the local kids thought of my brother and me as "the English" (this was definitely not a good thing in Wexford, where Oliver Cromwell massacred hundreds of the native people in 1649). When in England I was considered Irish (this was definitely not a good thing in my hometown of St Albans, which the terrorist provisional IRA had attacked in 1991 during their devastating campaign of bombings of British civilian targets).

I grew up at a time in a country where Gerry Adams (the president of the Irish Sinn Féin political party since 1983) was thought to be such a dangerous political presence that his voice was never broadcast on British television; his words were dubbed, instead, by an actor, as if his very voice was enough to incite rabid Irish Nationalist fervor in anyone who might be happening to be listening. Times have changed, of course; the Easter Peace Accords of 1998 have ushered in a far less violent era and an end to most of "The Troubles," while Adams and Sinn Féin have been welcomed into the political fold. However, to say I was culturally confused growing up would be an understatement, yet, as much as my Irishness was reviled in the UK and vice versa, I was to discover that the condition of Irish-Englishness also holds a strange power.

For my father, though, being purely Irish in the mid-twentieth century held little allure. He was born to a Catholic family in Bridgetown, Wexford, the fourth of five children, the year the Second World War ended. At that time the family farm had no electricity or running water. Though Irish and therefore not subject to conscription like a British citizen his father, Denis, had signed up for the British Navy; like W. B. Yeats's Irish Airman "no law or duty" bade him fight the Germans (though, of course, that Airman was Major Robert Gregory, killed in action in World War One, who came from a prominent Anglo-Irish family.) He served as an able seaman on HMS *Bellona,* and undertook several perilous Arctic convoys to besieged cities on the Baltic. He fought alongside the Americans off Arromanches between the Gold and Omaha beach landings; the USS *Texas,* which is now docked next to the San Jacinto monument only a few miles from my adopted home here in Houston, floated alongside the *Bellona,* strafing the German gun positions concealed in the white chalk cliffs behind canvas screens. Upon returning to Ireland he found not only the usual general state of penury but now the added insult of being treated like a traitor for fighting for the British, so he left, taking a job as a construction foreman on the massive rebuilding projects that were rising out of the smoking ruins of London.

In the late 1940s, the Connolly family took the boat train from Fishguard on the Welsh coast to the London terminus of Paddington Station. The area around the station at the time was almost entirely Irish. Apparently so wearied by the trip from the Old Country, they fell off the trains into the first rooming houses that would have them. This, remember, was at a time where lodgings would hang signs reading "No Blacks, No Dogs, No Irish" on the door. With his decent job Denis was able to secure one of the flats carved out of a prewar house that had survived the Blitz on Cambridge Square. There is, remarkably, film footage of my father from around this time. He's one of the street urchins in shorts lurking insalubriously around in the background in the Dirk Bogarde movie *The Blue Lamp* (1950), a police drama based at Paddington Green Station. Dad and his grimy band were paid for their work as extras with orange soda, an unimaginably exciting elixir in post-war London, where sugar, along with most everything else, was strictly rationed. When not providing background color for films, Dad and his gang spent most of their time running wild around the dangerous bombsites left by the aerial attacks on London, smashing up anything left behind that Hitler hadn't managed to annihilate already.

Though born in Ireland Dad felt mostly English with his London accent in contrast to the lilting Irish accents of his elder siblings. Certainly none of the neighbors made any attempt to conceal their distain for this little English boy when he returned "home" to Ireland (no matter how far or long you've been away it's always "home" in conversation with your Irish family and friends). Dad only got around to acquiring a British passport in 1979 in disgust at the provisional IRA's assassination of Lord Mountbatten; the last Viceroy of India was blown up by a bomb while on vacation along with members of his family on a boat off the coast of County Sligo, Ireland, while tending to the family lobster pots.

My father lost his Irish accent over the years but retains an Irish way of speaking. Sometimes it's Irish words and sounds: a "yoke" could mean any mechanical thing, from a wheelbarrow to a Boeing 747, and rather than ever being so bold as to agree with an outright "yes," he affirms things with a sharp intake of air as if he's just been winded. Most of all though it's this whimsical way of phrasing things that, somehow, owes something to the inflections of the Gaelic language that he never learned to speak, its trace absorbed by some strange sort of linguistic osmosis. This, of course, is the predicament that James Joyce's Stephen Dedalus finds himself in chapter five of *A Portrait of the Artist as a Young Man* when he considers his difficult relationship with the English language compared with the ease with which English Jesuit Dean of Studies at University College Dublin wields it:

> The language in which we are speaking is his before it is mine. How different are the words HOME, CHRIST, ALE, MASTER, on his lips and on mine! I cannot speak or write these words without unrest of spirit. His language, so familiar and so foreign, will always be for me an acquired speech. I have not made or accepted its words. My voice holds them at bay. My soul frets in the shadow of his language.

It's that fretting, that unrest of spirit, I think, that makes the Irish and, *particularly*, Irish-English such forces in the world of letters. Julian Moynahan argues in relation to the enduring appeal of Anglo-Irish writers that: "They may answer to our contemporary feeling of being at a loss in the world, of wanting more than anything to feel at home, while knowing our fate is homelessness. This appeal is to a very strange kind of nostalgia but not the less powerful for being so strange."

Yet this alienation is redoubled in the fate of the Irish-English. The nostalgia they have is for the very homeland they are already in. They are displaced by history, not space, and are often more dexterous with their adopted language than those that forced it on them. Yet, as we will see, the transatlantic passage often seems to cleanse the expatriate of the linguistic anxiety that so beleaguered Stephen Dedalus. This is very different from the loss of the Irish language in the American diaspora that Geraldine Connolly (no relation) writes of in "Our Mother Tongue," of how the Irish language became as transitory as snow, "the words / melting as they touched / the hard ground of a new land."

* * *

This Anglo-Irish / Irish-English division can also be illustrated in the world of American politics. All of the presidents of Irish extraction prior to John F. Kennedy's election to the office in 1961 were Protestant Anglo-Irish (or Scots-Irish, the term preferred in America since it was used to distinguish those earlier settlers from the waves of Catholic immigration in the wake of the Irish famines of the mid-nineteenth century). Kennedy was the first Irish Catholic. His family came during that period from Duganstown, Wexford, only 25 miles or so away as the crow flies from my family's place in Bridgetown. I was fascinated, upon coming to America as a Kennedy Scholar at Harvard University, with quite how differently being Irish is perceived in America, which, I think, is thanks in large part to the Kennedy family and their legacy.

The Kennedy Scholarship, established in 1965, is the British Government's living memorial to the memory of the assassinated president. Up to ten British students are year are awarded it in order to enable them to study at Harvard or MIT. I arrived at Logan airport in the summer of 2004 into the arms of my Irish relatives in Boston. Two of my grandfather's sisters had left impoverished Ireland for jobs in domestic service and the cotton mills of Massachusetts at about the same time as he left for London in the 1940s. Their families, now white-collar college-educated third-generation immigrants, generously welcomed me into their homes and lives. My own generation of cousins took me out drinking to the Irish pubs of Southie and Somerville and told me of their plans to return to live and work Ireland. I was perplexed. Why on earth would they leave all of the possibilities for advancement in America to go back to Ireland?

The last time I'd spent any time there, when I was a teenager in the early 1990s, it had been a miserable place: unemployment was running at about 16%, and many of my childhood friends already had unplanned kids thanks to the impossibility of acquiring contraception. At the time the only place to buy condoms in the entire country if you were under the age of 17 or unmarried was Richard Branson's Virgin Record Store in Dublin. The Irish government fined the company for doing so. Condoms were only made fully legal in Ireland in 1993, a full twelve years into the global AIDS epidemic. Most of my Irish cousins had fled the wretched place, scattering to the four corners of the world. This is why the IRA medals of Dennis Connolly, another great-uncle who fought against the British during the Irish war of Independence, came to be displayed in pride of place on an apartment wall in Bangkok. Since most of my family are in construction, many of them headed to Hong Kong to capitalize on the '90s building boom; Irish boys erecting bamboo scaffolding for enormous skyscrapers far higher than any buildings that existed in their native land. There is now a whole clan of Irish-Cantonese Connollys. By 2004, when my American cousins were considering moving back to the Old Country, the erstwhile "Celtic Tiger" economic boom that fueled growth due to foreign investment from the mid-90s was already cooling, and the bubble completely burst in 2008, casting Ireland's economy back to much the same terrible state it was in the early '90s. Those that ventured back to Ireland have now all returned to America, disillusioned.

My time in Boston was the first time I'd encountered the idea of Ireland and of being Irish as something appealing. This allure of Irishness is borne out by recent census data: those who claim Irish descent in America (34.5 million; and a further 5 million claim Scots-Irish roots) is seven times larger than the actual population of Ireland. Some of this, of course, is due to the huge waves of emigration from Ireland during the nineteenth-century famines and the mid-twentieth-century poverty, so harrowingly depicted in Frank McCourt's *Angela's Ashes*, that pushed my family out. Some of that number, however, must in part be due to a certain attraction to claiming an Irish identity. The Irish generally seem bemused by the tenuous claims to Irishness of the green beer-loving "plastic paddies" and are certainly grateful for the tourist dollars.

* * *

Far more than by my graduate research at Harvard, my American family seemed most excited by my new connection to the adored Kennedy clan that, I was to learn, had near-divine status in Boston. Teddy Kennedy was, prior to his death in 2009, much involved with the Kennedy scholarship and he invited each year's batch down to the Kennedy compound on the Cape. We arrived on a bright morning in May (it was my 29th birthday) to have a lobster lunch with the Senator and his wife Vicki before Teddy took all of the girls in the group (along with a malodourous Portuguese water spaniel called Splash, and contrary to the advice of parents everywhere) in his blue convertible into Hyannis to go look at the Kennedy Museum. People's reactions to him were extraordinary. One woman burst into hysterical tears lamenting the assassinations of Jack and Bobby. Teddy patiently consoled her on the death of his own brothers. This was as nothing compared to the reaction he would elicit when he showed us around Washington, D.C., over the Memorial Day weekend. He took us around the Senate and received us in his private offices, where he showed us an extraordinary Sectarian chessboard, divided up into green Nationalist and orange Loyalist squares. Carved political figures from both sides of the divide made up the pieces on the board. Later he took us to Arlington cemetery. We stood with him in front of his brothers' graves as crowds gathered and goggled aghast at the sight. It was a completely surreal and extremely moving experience.

My time at Harvard also afforded me the opportunity to meet Seamus Heaney, who was Ralph Waldo Emerson Poet-in-Residence there at the time. I was writing a chapter about the great man's elegies for other poets, and it was with enormous trembling trepidation that I knocked on his office door in the Barker Center. That anxiety was immediately dispelled by Heaney, whose demeanor was more that of a favorite Irish uncle than an imperious Nobel Laureate. Over the coming months he let me interview him multiple times, gave me draft versions and signed copies of his poems and paid for rounds of Guinness at the Plough and Stars on Massachusetts Avenue. One of the high points of my entire life was the Halloween evening that he gave a reading of his elegies for poets at the Harvard Advocate building, since, as he explained to the audience, they were much on his mind due to all my badgering. After the reading was finished we engaged in that most American of activities: carving pumpkin jack-o'-lanterns.

So how does America feature in poetic Heaney's Irish-Anglo imagination? The answer would appear to be very little. Despite spending a large part of the year in the States from 1979 to 2006, there are very few that directly address his American experience. "Bogland" (composed in 1968 before his first trip to the U.S. in 1969) is one of his first poems to include America, specifically the expanses of the vast West, in order to define Ireland by comparison: "We have no prairies here," "They'll never dig coal here." The poem ends with an image of "pioneers" but instead of the Western direction of manifest destiny or the transatlantic passage that preceded it, here their direction is downward as in "Digging" in the manifesto poem that he starts his debut collection, *Death of a Naturalist,* with:

> Our pioneers keep striking
> Inwards and downwards,
>
> Every layer they strip
> Seems camped on before.
> The bogholes might be Atlantic seepage.
> The wet centre is bottomless.

In *A Transnational Poetics* (2009) Jahan Ramazani seeks to deconstruct the "provincial" and "rooted" qualities usually ascribed to Irish poetry; those qualities so amusingly parodied in Billy Collins' "Irish Poetry" (I heard the ghost-clink of milk bottle / on the rough threshold / and understood the meadow-bells / that trembled over a nimbus of ragwort— / the whole afternoon lambent, corrugated, puddle-mad.") Ramazani argues that "postwar Irish poetry frequently transnationalizes the local.... the imaginative topography of Heaney's poetry is an intercultural space, a layered geography"; he is correct about the various layers of cultural accretion in Heaney's verse but it seems to me that the most fundamental layer, the bedrock of his imagination, is, always, Irish. Even in some of his most explicitly American poems America becomes the locus for reveries and nostalgia about Ireland. In "Westering: In California" we read of how Heaney "Recall[s] the last night / In Donegal, my shadow / Neat upon the whitewash" while in "Remembering Malibu" the "cold ascetic" of the Pacific is in "no way" as powerful as that of "our monk-fished, snowed-into Atlantic / no beehive hut for you / on the abstract sands of Malibu."

Images of traveling through snowy conditions feature frequently in Heaney's American poems. "In Iowa" Heaney travels through "a slathering blizzard, conveyed all afternoon / Through sleet-glit pelting hard against the windscreen," while in his first (uncollected) American poem "In an Airport Coach," Heaney writes of "The mouths of tunnels, / Fanged with icicles." Though undoubtedly America has more than its fair share of inclement weather it seems that the "snowed-into Atlantic" of Heaney's imagination is not that of the transatlantic trip to America but rather the one of return to Ireland, since the image powerfully resonates with the closing lines of James Joyce's "The Dead." The snow tapping on the window elicits an understanding in Gabriel Conroy that, "the time had come for him to set out on his journey westward." The snow that is "general all over Ireland," connects the civilized world of Dublin to the wilds of the west across the central "Bog of Allen and, father westward, softly falling into the dark mutinous Shannon waves."

Heaney's American imagination is often circumscribed by form as if to contain the experience of place. His progress through "the Badlands of New Jersey," in the poem "In an Airport Coach," are measured by an *aabccb* sextilla. "In Iowa" Heaney is contained both by the state and by the sonnet form (indeed, Iowa is a squarish sonnet-shaped state), while his "Villanelle for an Anniversary" (on the occasion of Harvard's 350th commencement) crams the references to the enormity of America advances and developments over the past four centuries or so—the expansion West, the Manhattan project, the moon landings—into Harvard Yard and the villanelle form. Contained thus America seems imaginatively and formally cordoned off from Heaney's Irish turf.

What of other recent transatlantic poetic traffic between Ireland and America? Certainly one can easily come up with several instances of American poets in Ireland: Robert Lowell living at the great Guinness mansion Castletown House in Kildare with his third wife Caroline Blackwood. He once hosted Seamus Heaney there, an event recalled in Heaney's "Pit Stop Near Castletown." The two poets "made our pit stop about half a mile / From the demesne gates, pissing like men / Together and apart against the wall." Also, John Berryman in Ireland on his 1966 Guggenheim scrawling *Dream Songs* in the pubs of Dublin to "have it out" with the shade of Yeats (according to Dream Song 312). I was delighted to learn that Berryman's frequent drinking companion was the singer Ronnie Drew of the Dubliners; surely the owners of two of the most resplendent and booze-soaked beards of the mid-twentieth century. More recently there has been an influx of extremely popular American poets into Ireland—including Billy Collins and Thomas Lynch—some of whom, one might imagine, may be attracted not only by the glorious landscape but also the Irish government's glorious tax exemption on monies earned from creative endeavors.

Though no tax relief for poets from the IRS, university posts are drawing the Irish to America: of course Heaney at Harvard, but also Paul Muldoon at Princeton, Thomas Kinsella at Temple, Seamus Deane at Berkeley, Greg Delanty at Saint Michael's College, and Eavan Boland at Stanford. What happens to the poetry of these deracinated poets? In particular, how do they fit with Derek Mahon's consideration of the difference between exile and expatriation: "It seems to me that an Englishman in France is an expat, but an Irishman is an exile"? Certainly this tension between expatriation and exile is what Boland is exploring in "Becoming Ann Bradstreet, "An Irish poet watching an English woman / Becoming an American poet." Muldoon, too, uses the test case of W. H. Auden, an English poet becoming American, in "7 Middagh Street"; but what of Irish poets becoming American?

Earlier Irish writers like Beckett and Joyce thought of themselves as aesthetic exiles. Indeed, Joyce concludes his great Dublin-based prose epic, *Ulysses* (1922) with an assertion of his own rootlessness in the hyphenated and peripatetic signoff on the final page "Trieste-Zurich-Paris, 1914–1921." Yet the Irish writer is not exiled in the manner, for example, of a political exile like Joseph Brodsky. The exile may be aesthetic or economic but there is always a homeland to which one might return. It seems also, increasingly, in our age of easy and relatively cheap transatlantic travel, that the idea of the exiled Irish writer can no longer hold up. Indeed, Heaney writes of exactly this ease of passage between the two places in "The Flight Path:"

> Jet-sitting next. Across and across and across.
> Westering, eastering, the jumbo a school bus
> 'The Yard' a cross between the farm and campus,
>
> A holding pattern and a tautening purchase—

I think it's that "tautening purchase" that we see increasingly in the poetry of the expatriated Irish in America: "purchase" suggesting both the hold and allure of the new world and the economic inducements for poets and academics to stay there. As Auden has it in his poem about American air travel "On the Circuit": "God bless the USA, so large / So friendly and so rich." There's also another sort of "purchase" going on: a linguist one whose hold operates differently between the Irish and the Irish-English.

* * *

I found myself at one of the most important outposts for Irish writing in America when I became Visiting Professor of British Literature at Wake Forest University in Winston-Salem, North Carolina, in 2006. For it is through the university press there that, as Helen Vendler explains, "Ireland comes to America." I was delighted to count two excellent contemporary Irish poets—Vona Groarke and Conor O'Callaghan—among my colleagues. I'll end now by considering the first of two poems entitled "Away" from Groarke's 2006 collection

Spindrift, for though Groarke is entirely Irish, her poems resonate profoundly with my own expatriated Irish-English experience.

The very idea of being "Away," of course, suggests a kind of temporary expatriation where the homeland is always implied by being physically away from it. Whereas in Heaney's work being in America prompts reveries of Ireland, for Groarke a different dynamic is at play, as Ireland becomes Americanized. In the first stanza of her "Away" poem, her home in Winston-Salem is defined by its very un-Irishness; the thatch and whitewash of Irish cliché replaced with American architectural features such as a "crawl space" and a "stoop." Her description of her commute, "flitting through every amber / between Gales and Drumcliffe Road" seemed, on first reading, almost too serendipitous to be true. I certainly couldn't recall a "Drumcliffe Road" after spending two years living in Winston-Salem prior to moving to Houston in 2008. Yet there it is on the map. Drumcliffe, of course, is the name of the cemetery in which W. B. Yeats is buried in County Sligo in the west of Ireland. Yeats described his own gravesite and dictated his own epitaph in "Under Ben Bulben," leaving behind the imperious instructions, "Irish poets learn your trade / Sing whatever is well made" so "That we in coming days may be / Still the indomitable Irishry." Here Groarke, plying her trade in America, has found this most Irish of place names replanted on North Carolinian soil; no longer an end point but a way through.

Other images of Americanized Irishness appear. She paints her house's woodwork "the exact azure / of a wave's flipside / out the back of Spiddal pier," while morning pins a "swatch of sunlight / to my purple shamrock plant." The very emblem of Irishness—the shamrock—a different color here and bathed in unaccustomed light. The green of the shamrock is to be found not in her garden but embedded, instead, in the ubiquitous name of a pharmacy:

> Yesterday
> I answered in a class of Irish
> at the checkout of Walgreen's.

> I walk through the day-to-day
> as if ferrying a pint glass
> filled to the brim with water
>
> that spills into my own accent:
> pewtered, dim, far-reaching
> lost for words.

She's not teaching "a class of Irish" to her students at Wake Forest; rather her Americanized and diluted accent has become a new "class of Irish" accent. For the Irish-English, conflicted and confused in Ireland or Britain, there is strange solace to be had in this. The linguistic anxiety that Groarke seems to feel in relation to the encroachment and dilution of her own Irishness is a comfort to the "inner émigré" status of Irish-Englishness that Heaney interrogates in his poem "Exposure."

Heaney expanded upon his well-known formulation in a 1998 interview with George Morgan, explaining: "When I said 'inner émigré,' I meant to suggest a state of poetic stand-off, as it were, a state where you have slipped out of your usual social persona and have entered more creatively and fluently into your inner being." Heaney achieved this initially with his move to Ireland, by becoming Irish-English. The American expatriation of the "inner émigré" enables that poetic stand-off yet further; enabling one to slip the bonds of being contrary and conflicted, and finding oneself afresh in the "holding pattern and a tautening purchase" of the American experience.

* * *

I live and work in Houston, Texas, now: a town of expatriates, a twenty-first-century Ellis Island of the documented and undocumented, polyglot and immense, the most diverse city in America. People guess at my increasingly transatlantic accent all day: Australian? Scottish maybe? Nobody cares if I'm Irish or English, since most everyone is from someplace else. We are all as equally exotic and ordinary as the other. Those Iberian "black Irish" genes mean I am addressed in Spanish as frequently as I am in English. My children Elizabeth (named after the Irish grandmother) and Seamus (named after the Irish poet) hold British and American citizenship and are listed on the Irish Leabhar Taifeadta Breitheanna Coigríche (Register of Foreign Births). They sport an extraordinary Texan drawl, vowels crammed into words, eddying like Joyce's in *Finnegans Wake,* until I can barely understand what they're saying. I'm happy here, no longer contrary or conflicted. I'm home.

An A—Z of Seamus Heaney

Aarhaus: In his poem "The Tollund Man" (*Wintering Out*, 1972) Heaney writes, "Some day I will go to Aarhaus / To see his peat-brown head, / the mild pods of his eye-lids, / His pointed skin cap." The Tollund Man was an Iron Age human sacrifice near-perfectly preserved in the Jutland peat and subsequently excavated and studied by the Danish archeologist P. V. Glob. Heaney made the pilgrimage to Aarhaus in 1973 and came face-to-face with the Tollund Man in the Silkeborg museum along with other preserved sacrificial victims such as the Grauballe Man and the Windeby Girl. Glob's book about these finds, *The Bog People,* was profoundly influential for Heaney, for in it he found "befitting emblems of adversity" (a phrase he took from Yeats) for the sectarian and internecine violence of contemporary Northern Ireland that he was to write about in his 1975 collection North.

Bellaghy: location of the recently opened Seamus Heaney HomePlace museum and site of his final resting place. Heaney died in a Dublin hospital on 30 August 2013. He sent his last words (*Noli timere*—Latin for "Don't be afraid") in a text to his wife Marie. Heaney was buried in Bellaghy graveyard alongside many of his family members three days later, after a funeral service in Dublin. His epitaph reads "WALK ON AIR AGAINST YOUR BETTER JUDGMENT," a quote taken from his nostalgic and instructive poem "The Gravel Walks." It is notably far more encouraging (as epitaphs go) than W. B. Yeats's stern command to "Cast a cold eye/ On life, on death/ Horseman, pass by."

County Derry: One of Northern Ireland's six counties (the others are Antrim, Armagh, Down, Fermanagh, and Tyrone) and the place of Heaney's birth on April 13, 1939 to Patrick Heaney (a farmer and cattle trader) and Margaret McCann. Unlike the other counties, Derry functions as a verbal sectarian marker between the two major political factions. Nationalists (those Catholics who wish to reunite Northern Ireland with the Republic of Ireland) refer to the area as Derry while

Unionists (those Protestants who wish to remain part of the United Kingdom) use "Londonderry." Heaney was born to a Catholic family north of the border so would always use the term "Derry."

Dublin: Heaney moved his family there to the suburb of Sandymount in 1976 after four happy years in Wicklow (Sandymount Strand is, of course, where the "Proteus" chapter of James Joyce's *Ulysses* takes place). Other than stints as a professor in America it would remain his home until his death in 2013. Though he spent lots of time there, Dublin scarcely features in his poetry at all.

Éire: the Republic of Ireland. In 1916 the Irish Proclamations of the Republic asserted Ireland's independence from the United Kingdom and lead to the Irish War of Independence (1919–1921) against British rule. The Irish Free State was founded as a dominion of the British Commonwealth in 1922 (Northern Ireland opted out of joining the South in one united nation), the Irish constitution was established in 1937 and Irealnd became a Republic in 1949. Though Heaney was born in Northern Ireland and was therefore a British subject he moved south of the border in 1972 and renounced his British citizenship for Irish. In "Open Letter," a verse riposte to his inclusion in an anthology of British poets, he writes. 'Be advised, my passport's green / No glass of ours was ever raised / To toast the Queen' (British passports were, at the time, blue, then becames European red, and are now, thanks to Brexit, about to return to blue again).

Francis Ledwidge (1887–1917): Heaney included a fine elegy for this early twentieth-century Irish poet in *Field Work* (1979). Ledwidge and Heaney share a pastoral appreciation of the Irish landscape in their poems. He was a Catholic who signed up to fight in the British Army against the Germans during World War One (1914–1918) but as the War drew on he grew disillusioned. His dilemma was (as Heaney quotes from one of Ledwidge's own letters of June 1917 in the poem), "'To be called a British soldier while my country / Has no place among nations'." Ledwidge was killed in action on 31 July 1917.

Glanmore: A small village in County Wicklow some 30 miles south of Dublin as the crow flies. Heaney and his wife moved to the cottage in Glanmore with their three children (Michael, Christopher, and Catherine Ann) in the summer of 1972. Heaney spent four happy and prolific years writing in there, including, of course, "Glanmore Sonnets," which are dedicated to Ann Saddlemyer, who rented them the cottage. In 1988 Heaney bought the cottage from Saddlemyer and wrote many of his Oxford lectures there. As Heaney explained, Glanmore, "saved my creative life. Sandymount [in Dublin] is where my domestic life is lived, but Glanmore is where my imaginative existence feels guaranteed. I work more confidently and more productively there than anywhere else."

Harvard: Heaney worked as a visiting professor at Harvard University from 1979 and was appointed to be the Boylston Professor of Rhetoric and Oratory from 1984 to 1995. After that time he served as the Ralph Waldo Emerson poet-in-residence until 2006. While at Harvard, Heaney was affiliated with, and lived at, Adams House. His "Villanelle for an Anniversary" was composed for Harvard's three hundred and fiftieth commencement.

Incertus: Heaney's pseudonym on starting to publish poems in the early 1960s. Latin for "uncertain." Heaney writes about his *nom de poésie* in his prose poem "Incertus" (Stations, 1975),

> I went disguised in it, pronouncing it with a soft church-Latin c, tagging it under my efforts like a damp fuse. Uncertain. A shy soul fretting and all that. Expert obeisance.

> Oh yes, I crept before I walked. The old pseudonym lies there like a mouldering tegument.

In many ways this ability to embrace uncertainty and ambivalence was to become one of the defining features of Heaney's *oeuvre*. In "Exposure" Heaney writes tellingly of his conflicted state: "I am neither internee nor informer; / An inner émigré."

James Joyce (1882–1941): Though a prose writer rather than a poet, Joyce is an unavoidable though relatively benign influence in Heaney's work. He functions much like Virgil to Heaney's Dante at the close of "Station Island" (*Station Island,* 1984) where a blind, familiar figure with an ashplant walking stick tells Heaney, "Keep at a tangent. / When they make the circle wide, it's time to swim // out on your own and fill the element / with signatures on your own frequency." We find the presence of Joyce once more in "The Granite Chip" (*Electric Light,* 2001), the titular chip a memento "hammered off Joyce's Martello / Tower" in Sandycove. The chip, "flecked insoluble brilliant" with "Jaggy, salty punitive // and exacting" qualities, is a symbol of what Joyce stands for in Heaney's mind, an object which he feels simultaneously attached to, yet alienated from: "I keep but feel little in common with."

Kenning: A compound poetic phrase, characteristic of Old English verse and frequently used as a device by Heaney. For example, "word-hoard," "bone-house," "treasure-seat" and, in "Glanmore Sonnets" a series of kennings to describe the sea: "eel-road, / seal-road, keel-road, whale-road."

London: Heaney was far fonder of the city than one might expect from someone who had renounced their British citizenship. He and Marie Devlin honeymooned there after their wedding in 1965 (a happy time described in his poem "The Underground," *Station Island,* 1984). The London Underground also provided the title of his penultimate collection of poetry *District and Circle* (2006).

Mossbawn: The three-roomed whitewashed thatched family farm in Derry where Heaney was born and grew up as the eldest of nine siblings. The name of the farm is freighted with meaning for Heaney as he explains in his prose collection *Preoccupations* (1980): "Our farm was called Mossbawn. *Moss,* a Scots word probably carried to Ulster by the Planters, and *bawn,* the name the English colonists gave to their fortified farmhouses. Mossbawn the planter's house of the bog. Yet in spirit of this Ordnance Survey spelling, we pronounced it Moss bann, and *bán* is the Gaelic word for white. So might not the thing mean the white moss, the moss of bog-cotton? In the syllables of my home I see a metaphor of the split culture of Ulster."

Nobel Prize: Seamus Heaney was awarded the Nobel Prize for Literature in 1995. The other Irish winners of the prize are W. B. Yeats, George Bernard Shaw and Samuel Beckett. Heaney was on holiday in Greece at the time and did not learn of news until he phoned home the day after the announcement. As the Irish poet Lachlan Mckinnon noted "he seemed to take the Nobel as an encouragement rather than a reward." In his Nobel lecture "Crediting Poetry" Heaney writes of his formative encounters with language: "the child in the bedroom listening simultaneously to the domestic idiom of his Irish home and the official idioms of the British broadcaster while picking up from behind both the signals of some other distress, that child was already being schooled for the complexities of his adult predicament, a future where he would have to adjudicate among promptings variously ethical, aesthetical, moral, political, metrical, skeptical, cultural, topical, typical, post-colonial and, taken all together, simply impossible."

Oxford: Seamus Heaney served as the Oxford Professor of Poetry from 1989 to 1994. A collection of the lectures he gave in that capacity, were published by Oxford University Press in 1990 as *The Redress of Poetry*. In his preface to a reprint of the lectures he comments, with characteristic modesty, "since the experience of lecturing ... was not only honorific but daunting, it was always a relief to meet the supportive faces that one had met in the audience again, after the event, in the bar of the East Gate Hotel: bitter has never tasted sweeter."

Plough and Stars: Pub in Cambridge, Massachusetts often frequented by Heaney while at Harvard. Takes its name from a play by Seán O'Casey first produced at the Abbey Theatre in Dublin in 1926 about the 1916 Easter Uprising.

Queen's University, Belfast: The foremost university of Northern Ireland, located in its capital Belfast. Heaney attended Queen's

University as an undergraduate and took a first-class degree in English Literature in 1961. He was appointed as a lecturer at Queens in 1966 and taught there until 1970, when he was offered a visiting position at Berkeley for a year. Upon returning to Belfast Heaney grew disillusioned with living in Northern Ireland, and wrote an article called "Belfast's Black Christmas" in *The Listener* magazine in December 1971, which described his experience of living in the divided city: "This morning I was stopped on the Falls Road and marched to the nearest police barracks, with my three-year-old son, because my car tax was out of date. My protests grew limp when the officer in charge said: 'Look, either you go to the police station up the road or we take you now to Holywood'—their own ground." He moved south to the Republic of Ireland in 1972. Queens University is now the home of the Seamus Heaney Centre for Poetry.

Rossville Street: The site in Derry City of the Bloody Sunday Massacre on 30 January 1972 and location of the Bloody Sunday monument. The massacre occurred when British paramilitaries fired on unarmed civilians, killing 14. The event was one of the bloodiest chapters in the era of sectarian violence (that were euphemistically referred to as "The Troubles") that ran from the late 1960s until the Good Friday Peace accords in 1998. Heaney writes about the incident in his poem "Casualty" (*Field Work*, 1979) an elegy for a Catholic fisherman friend of his killed in a pub bombing a few days after the massacre:

> He was blown to bits
> Out drinking in a curfew
> Others obeyed, three nights
> After they shot dead
> The thirteen men in Derry.
> PARAS THIRTEEN, the walls said,
> BOGSIDE NIL.

Thole: An Old English word for "lament" that Heaney describes as a "loophole" and way into a "further language" in his preface to *Beowulf* (2000).

Sweeney: protagonist of the old Irish poem *Buile Shuibhne* (Sweeney's Madness) in which Suibhne mac Colmain is cursed by St Ronan and driven to insanity. Heaney translated the work as *Sweeney Astray* (1983). Heaney has translated many works from several languages, including sections of Dante's *Inferno*, the whole of the Old English epic *Beowulf*, an interpretation of Sophocles's *Antigone* entitled *The Burial At Thebes* (2004) and the Irish poem "A School of Poetry Closes: Tadhg Og O'huiginn's Lament for his master and brother, Fergal Rua."

Uisce beatha: Gaelic for "water of life" aka whiskey. Irish whiskey is always spelled with an "e" and Scottish whisky omits it. Heaney's favored tipple of choice was Bushmills.

Ventry: A small coastal village on the barren Dingle peninsula, one of the westernmost places in Europe, in County Kerry. The remote and now-abandoned Blasket Islands (Na Blascaodaí) sit off the coast of the Dingle peninsula and feature in Heaney's poem "The Given Note" (*Door into the Dark*, 1969). Ventry features in Heaney's poem "Shoreline," which lists the names of various coastal towns on the Irish landmass to illustrate the psychogeography of place and history embedded in their syllables: "Strangford, Arklow, Carrickfergus / Belmullet and Ventry / Stay, forgotten like sentries."

Word-Hoard: one of Heaney's most frequent and most telling kennings. Heaney repeatedly draws on the idea of a trans-national and trans-historic linguistic treasure trove. Of course, as explored in his Nobel lecture, this sensitivity to language has something to do with the condition of Irish-Englishness. In "Station Island" the shade of Joyce warns Heaney off his frustration with the English language of those who suppressed the Gaelic of the native Irish in Northern Ireland "'Who cares,' / he jeered , 'any more? The English language / belongs to us. You are raking at dead fires.'" Of course, this is exactly the frustration that Joyce's Stephen Dedalus expresses in his diary entries at the close of *A Portrait of the Artist a Young Man*. His entry for April 13 (Heaney's birthday) reads. "That tundish has been on my mind for a long time. I looked it up and find it English and good old blunt English too. Damn the dean of studies and his funnel! What did he come here for to teach us his own language or to learn it from us. Damn him one way or the other!"

X: Tricky one, this. In "Clearances," a series of poems in memory of his mother, he writes of playing a game of Noughts & Crosses with her (the British English for Tic-Tac-Toe) "In moves where I was X and she was O." If Margaret's lack of presence in death is prefigured in the poem in the nothingness of the game's nought, the "x" marks the spot where we can find the poet in his poem.

Yeats: Though W. B. Yeats (1865–1939), Heaney tends to deal with his great poetic precursor in prose rather than in his poetry, where references to him are brief and glancing. Heaney is far more at home in his poetry in the company of other Irish influences such as Joyce and Patrick Kavanagh (1904–1967). When asked by the author about this tendency to avoid the Yeatsian in his work, Heaney commented that Yeats functioned in his poetic imagination, "like a mountain range in the offing, lying there, there's no way I can address Yeats in any way. It's like an English poet addressing Shakespeare, with Yeats it's like a finished deposit. It's perfect in the Latin sense, it's done. I can't imagine Yeats being addressed."

Zbigniew Herbert (1924–1988): A Polish poet, who, along with his fellow countryman Czesław Miłosz (1911–2004) exerted a profound moral influence upon Heaney's work. There is a poem "To the Shade of Zbigniew Herbert" in *Electric Light* that consists of the final six lines of a 1998 sonnet on the poet originally entitled "Hyperborean." The shorter edited poem takes on a far more valedictory and epitaphic quality and focuses on the appeal that these "hyperborean" poets had to Heaney.

> You were the one of those from the back of the north wind
> Whom Apollo favoured and would keep going back to
> In the winter season. And among your people you
> Remained his herald whenever he'd departed
> And the land was silent and summer's promise thwarted.
> You learnt the lyre from him and kept it tuned.

The same could be said of Heaney, the poet from and of the North, too.

Two Genealogical Elegies for Seamus Heaney

I have coined the termed "genealogical elegies" for poems occasioned by the death of poets rather than calling such poems "professional elegies" in the manner of some recent critics such as Sara Jamieson and Jahan Ramazani. In doing so, it is not my intention to invoke moral philosophy or the ghosts of Nietzsche and Foucault (although I do agree with the latter when he writes that "Genealogy ... operates on a field of entangled and confused parchments, on documents that have been scratched over and recopied many times"). In family genealogies, descendants have little say in their progenitors' identity and can only dutifully trace their lineage in retrospect (which is why Michel Foucault also asserts that genealogy "is gray, meticulous, and patiently documentary" while these poems are anything but). Genealogical elegists, in contrast, adopt their own poetic parents, forge (sometimes in both senses) their own poetic lineage, and reveal an acquisition of influence by selecting which forebears to address in their elegies.

Often what is at stake in genealogical elegy is not the fate of the dead poet's reputation but rather that of the living as the elegist makes canon fodder of the dead. Rather than just consoling the living, such poems also seek to challenge them if the living also happen to be fellow poets. These poems also continually revisit the *locus horridus* of anxiety over the centrality (or rather, the lack thereof) of poetry in society. Thus, genealogical elegy is concerned not only with the death of the poet but also with the possible death of poetry itself.

One of the oldest tropes in elegy is that of the inefficacy of language when faced with inexpressibly awful loss. Nowhere is this more pronounced than in those poets, through whom, as W. H. Auden writes in his elegy for W. B. Yeats, language lives. For, as Joseph Brodsky argues in *Less than One,* the death of a poet is "something more than a human loss. Above all, it is a drama of language." David Kennedy goes on to consider this drama in his book *Elegy,* explaining, "in the case of elegies for poets, one individual's poetry continues because another's cannot. Elegy is therefore in its own way a species of enquiry into limits and into how to pass through an originary aporia. This, in turn, helps to reveal elegy as an overt dramatization of issues of representability and non-representability that underwrite all poetry." The theoretical course I chart here will consider what "species of enquiry" two genealogical elegies for Seamus Heaney undertake and how these elegists dramatize the effect of Heaney's death on poetry and language. Aporia, of course, literally means to be without a way through, lacking a passage; genealogical elegy foregrounds form and the craft of making in order to provide a way though this "originary aporia."

Paul Muldoon's "Cuthbert and the Otters," an elegy for Heaney after his death in the summer of 2013, was commissioned for the Durham Literary festival. This took place at Durham Cathedral, which holds St Cuthbert's tomb (his relics were moved to Durham from Linsfarne Island, Northumbria, after it was sacked by Danes in 875). It first appeared in the *Times Literary Supplement* of December 20, 2013 and begins with a scene in St Cuthbert's cell on Lindsfarne:

> Notwithstanding the fact that one of them has gnawed a strip of flesh
> from the shoulder of the salmon,
> relieving it of a little darne,
> the fish these six otters would fain
> carry over the sandstone limen
> and into Cuthbert's cell, a fish garlanded with bay leaves
> and laid out on a linden-flitch

Starting with "Notwithstanding" —a portmanteau word of refutation as odd as the disappearance of Yeats in the first line of Auden's "In Memory of W. B. Yeats"—draws attention to Muldoon's linguistic agenda in the elegy, an agenda that is immediately underscored by the arcane and archaic end words "darne," "fain," "limen," and "flitch." St Cuthbert (CE 634–687), the Bishop of Lindsfarne, is best known to us thanks to the Venerable Bede's hagiographic accounts of the *Life of St Cuthbert* in both verse and prose. Bede tells of how, after spending the night praying while immersed in the North Sea, Cuthbert staggered back ashore accompanied by two otters who dried him with their pelts and warmed him with their breath. In the poem the kindly otters have multiplied threefold and brought the bishop his (nearly intact) supper. Here it is the fish that wears the laurels, not Cuthbert, and we may wonder why Muldoon chose the figure of Cuthbert the priest as a point of reference to commemorate Heaney the poet, aside from the fact that the poem was commissioned to be read at Cuthbert's final resting place.

Though not an artist himself, Cuthbert's life inspired what is undoubtedly one of the greatest acts of artistry in human history: the creation of the illuminated Lindsfarne Gospels in the early eight century. This was a project undertaken by Cuthbert's successor as bishop of Lindsfarne to glorify the new saint. Cuthbert is also a particularly suitable figure in relation to Heaney, since he stands for the kind of condition of Anglo-Irishness that we find Heaney grappling with repeatedly in his verse thirteen centuries later. Cuthbert was educated in the Irish church (several scholars have gone so far as to speculate that he was also born in Ireland) and became a central figure in the history of Celtic Christianity. The only direct parallel that Muldoon draws, however, between the two men is geographical: "The floor of Cuthbert's cell is flush // with the floor of Ballynahone Bog after the first Autumn rains." Ballynahone Bog is very close to Heaney's final resting place, the town of Bellaghy, in County Derry, while "from Durham to Desertmartin" (30) links the location of Cuthbert's tomb with a village in Derry close to Heaney's birthplace. This twinning of places in the poem draws together not only the two men but also the complicated history of northern Europe, just as Heaney had done in his own collection North (which parallels the violent sacrificial killings of stone age Jutland with the present-day Troubles in Northern Ireland). Muldoon's choice of the tale of St. Cuthbert and the otters also echoes Heaney's "St Kevin and the Blackbird" (on the relationship between a saint and an animal) and his love poem "The Otter." In one of the lectures he gave during his tenure as the Oxford Professor of Poetry, Muldoon argues that Heaney's Field Work is profoundly informed by Robert Lowell, and in particular, his translation of Eugenio Montale's "The Eel," and that this Lowellian influence is most apparent in "The Otter." Consequently Muldoon's choice of Heaney's otter "Heavy and frisky, in your freshened pelt, / Printing the stones" to figure so heavily in his genealogical elegy not only alludes to Heaney's own poetry but also indicates the significance of Lowell's legacy in Heaney's work.

The first stanza of "Cuthbert and the Otters" also establishes the unrhymed septet stanza form that will be Muldoon's pattern throughout. This is not the rhyme royal of Chaucer's *Troilus and Criseyde*, but rather a form far closer to the one suggested by Heaney's own recent looser translation of *The Testament of Cresseid* (2009) by the sixteenth-century Scottish makar Robert Henryson. Here Muldoon adopts Heaney's own formal innovation, that "kind of valediction" Heaney himself paid to dead poets: his appropriation of pre-modern works in his own translation and in their memory. As Auden alluded not only to Yeats but also Shakespeare, Blake and Tennyson in the tetrameter quatrains of the final part of "In Memory of W. B. Yeats," here Muldoon formally gestures toward Chaucer and Henryson by way of Heaney's translation. There is also a further significant association: Chaucer and Henryson, were, of course, both poets that Dunbar enshrined for posterity in his "Lament for the Makaris."

This kind of allusion at one remove is characteristic of the way in which Muldoon's genealogical elegy operates and the poem is a dizzyingly associative welter and web of images, words, people and places. The passage of centuries collapses under the weight of transhistorical connections as we find Viking Danes that "are already dyeing everything beige. / In anticipation, perhaps, of the carpet and mustard factories" of the modern North of England; while we read of how "Irish monasticism may well derive from Egypt."[1] The most significant connection that Muldoon draws, however, is between Old English and the language spoken by Heaney as he explores exactly the same kind of Anglo-Celtic linguistic frisson that Heaney read into his portentous birthday in his "Station Island" sequence. As Heaney explains to the shade of another, James Joyce, whom he encounters at

---

1. This is the thesis of Gregory Telepneff's *The Egyptian Desert in the Irish Bogs: The Byzantine Character of Early Celtic Monasticism.*

the close of his pilgrimage around the island, his birthday corresponds with a highly significant date in twentieth-century literature:

> there is a moment in Stephen's diary
> for April the thirteenth, a revelation
>
> set among my stars—that one entry
> has been a sort of password in my ears,
> the collect of a new epiphany,
> the Feast of the Holy Tundish.

It is on this day in Joyce's *A Portrait of the Artist as a Young Man* (1916) that Stephen Dedalus records his indignation at being rebuked by a dean at University College Dublin for using the word "tundish" to mean "funnel," a usage that the master tells Stephen is Irish and uneducated. In response, Stephen writes, "That tundish has been on my mind for a long time. I looked it up and find it in English and good old blunt English too. Damn the dean of studies and his funnel! What did he come here for to teach us his own language or to learn it from us. Damn him one way or the other!"

"Cuthbert and the Otters" echoes with words that function much like Stephen Dedalus's tundish—hauberkerd, lief, skald—that draw attention to the genealogy of the English language from which the poem is made. For example, Muldoon finds himself "at once full of dread / and in complete denial" explaining in the alexandrine line that will become the poem's elegiac refrain "I cannot thole the thought of Seamus Heaney dead." Muldoon's choice of the archaic Old English "thole" in a line which will go on to become the elegy's refrain enacts the project of making and connecting, while, at the same time, describing Muldoon's desolation as he struggles to connect the dots and make in the vacuum left by Heaney's sudden death.

"Thole" functions as a kind of controlling allusion for the entirety of the poem since the word has profound significance for Heaney. As we learn in his introduction to his translation of *Beowulf* (2001), he thinks of it as a kind of linguistic "loophole" and "entry into a further language":

I found in the glossary to C. L. Wrenn's edition of the poem the Old English word meaning 'to suffer,' the word *þolian;* and although at first it looked completely strange with its thorn symbol instead of the familiar *th*, I gradually realized that it was not strange at all, for it was the word that older and less educated people would have used in the country where I grew up. 'They'll just have to learn to thole,' my aunt would say about some family who had suffered an unforeseen bereavement. And now suddenly here was "thole" in the official textual world, mediated through the apparatus of a scholarly edition, a little bleeper to remind me that my aunt's language was not just a self-enclosed family possession but an historical heritage, one that involved the journey *þolian* had made north into Scotland and then across into Ulster with the planters and then across from the planters to the locals who had originally spoken Irish and then farther across again when the Scots Irish emigrated to the American South in the eighteenth century. When I read in John Crowe Ransom the line 'Sweet ladies, long may ye bloom, and toughly I hope ye may thole,' my heart lifted again, the world widened, something was furthered. The far-flungness of the word, the phenomenological pleasure of finding it variously transformed by Ransom's modernity and *Beowulf*'s venerability made me feel vaguely something for which again I only found the words years later. What I was experiencing as I kept meeting up with *thole* in its multicultural odyssey was the feeling, which Osip Mandelstam once defined as a 'nostalgia for world culture.' And this was a nostalgia I didn't even know I suffered until I experience its fulfillment in this little epiphany. It was as if, on the analogy of a baptism by desire, I had undergone something like illumination by philology. And even though I did not know it at the time, I had by then reached the point where I was ready to translate *Beowulf. Polian* had opened my right-of-way.

We too share in this kind of "illumination by philology" as we read "Cuthbert and the Otters" but it is not as simple as the right-of-way *polian* affords Heaney. Rather Muldoon is invested in not only exposing our linguistic heritage but also revealing the instability of the medium of his making, in doing so making his own contribution to the feedback loop of the genre of genealogical elegy.

For a poem that is so aware of constriction (the "limen" of the cell and Muldoon "hemmed in" by sorrow) and the constraints of elegiac convention (as one point we read of how "refrain" comes from "*frenulum,* 'a bridle'"), Muldoon's elegy is, in many ways, surprisingly traditional. There are laurels (the fish "garlanded with bay leaves"); an elegiac refrain ("I cannot thole the thought of Seamus Heaney dead"); there is a description of the procession of mourners and the final line of the poem even attains a form of consoling stellification ("Reflugent all. From *Fulgere,* 'to flash'") even as it alludes to Shelley's description of untimely death in "Adonais" (those "extinct in their refulgent prime"). That etymological impulse apparent in his gloss on the refrain and in the poem's closing line is the greatest innovation of this genealogical elegy, for language itself becomes the muse that Muldoon interrogates.

As R. Clifton Spargo argues in *The Ethics of Mourning,* "It is often supposed that since mourning traces the gaps, aporias, or chasms of language, the real cultural work of literary grief is to mend the rift between language and meaning that develops from the perspective of one who experiences a great loss." Muldoon resists this linguistic closure as he disrupts elegiac language by a variety of strategies. We can find examples of parapraxsis and self-correction ("Did I say 'calamine?' / I meant 'chamomile'" as the heard verbal slip becomes a written made thing that reveals language's instability. Muldoon plays with the structure of analogical reasoning—"Coffin is to truckle / as salmon is to catafalque"—to demonstrate how easily our associative impulses are led astray. We can also find homophones that reveal the imprecision of the spoken word—"flitch," "filched," "fletch," and "the way we swap 'scuttle' for 'scupper'"—and even implied homophones. "Fain" would the otters carry the salmon, and while the "Irish war band" (the Gaelic *fian* that has "has 27 members") is never actually named it is structurally central the poem though since Muldoon allows himself as many stanzas in the elegy as men in the *fian.*) This functions as a kind of productive Oulipoian constraint as

Heaney is enshrined into the pantheon of Celtic warriors through Muldoon's form.

One of the most striking aspects of the poem is how, on first reading, it may seem rather impersonal as the friendship between the two poets (they first met in 1968 when Heaney was 28 and Muldoon 16) is obscured behind the poem's huge frame of reference. It is with some surprise that we recognize both Heaney and Muldoon's physical presence in the world of poem:

> What looks like a growth of stubble
> has to do with the chin drying out. I straighten my
> black tie as the pall-bearer
>
> who almost certainly filched
> that strip of skin draws level with me.

The shock of the presence of Heaney's corpse in the poem (like the shock of the open casket at Catholic funerals) with its stubble still growing will go on later in the poem to compel Muldoon into repeating his elegiac refrain, "As with the stubble, so with the finger and toenails. / I cannot thole the thought of Seamus Heaney dead." The enjambment across the stanza break enforces the surprise that it is the hungry otter that bears Heaney's coffin rather Muldoon. Well not yet, but "Halfway through what's dissolved into the village // of Bellaghy, this otter steps out from under the bier / and offers me his spot."

This is a maneuver akin to that which Muldoon identifies at the close of Heaney's own "Elegy" for Lowell, the two men saying goodbye under the bay tree at the Heaney's house in Glanmore, Ireland, a few days before Lowell's death in New York City, the laurels passing from one to the other. The acquisition of influence here is unmistakable as we read of how Muldoon wants "that coffin to cut a notch // in my clavicle" and of how "Irish-Americans still hold a dirge-chanter / in the highest esteem. That, and to stand in an otter's stead." Muldoon, chanting his dirge in the otter's stead takes something from the Laureate Heaney just as surely as the otter takes the darne—a juicy morsel—from the bay-wreathed salmon in the poem's first stanza. What Muldoon filches is Heaney's "thole" and the "nostalgia for world culture" that his encounters with that word created in him. It is this nostalgia rather than consolation that Muldoon's genealogical elegy evokes as the earth of Bellaghy receives its honored guest.

It is exactly this kind of "nostalgia for world culture" that John Matthias considers in his "Elegy for Seamus Heaney," but rather than a word providing the ingress as was the case with Muldoon, instead we find a form: the familiar pulse of the rhymed tetrameter quatrains from the final part of W. H. Auden's "In Memory of W. B. Yeats." Though this final section is often (and convincingly) scanned as catalectic trochaic tetrameter (for example, here in the first lines: "EARTH re | CEIVE an | HONoured | GUEST, / WILLiam | YEATS is | LAID to | REST"), it is also possible to reverse the metrical pattern and read it as acephalous iambic tetrameter instead: "EARTH | reCEIVE | an HON | oured GUEST, / WILL | iam YEATS | is LAID | to REST" (42–43). (I am indebted to Charles O. Hartman for pointing out the latter possibility to me.) Auden's is a Janus-faced form casting simultaneously backward and forward in a section of the poem that inters the body of one of the previous generation's poets while importuning the poets of a coming generation.

Auden underscores the notion of the poem as a made thing in "In Memory of W. B. Yeats" by foregrounding inherited forms through the rigid beat that hammers throughout the quatrains of the final section. These stanzas, of course, metrically echo both the abba quatrains of the first part of Shakespeare's "The Phoenix and the Turtle" and the aabb quatrains of Blake's "The Tyger" but Auden transmutes this shape into something especially elegiac and authoritative. Shakespeare's imperative "Let" ("Let the bird of loudest lay," "Let the priest in surplice white"), becomes an allowance accorded specifically to poetry and poets ("Let the Irish vessel lie / Emptied of its poetry," "Let the healing fountain [i.e. poetry] start"). The solemn trochaic beat Auden establishes as an elegiac form in this poem pulses through twentieth century elegies for poets—for example in Brodsky's elegy for T. S. Eliot and Heaney's for Brodsky—as a shorthand for poetic indebtedness.

Matthias does not merely repeat Auden's form but rather extends the consideration in which Heaney himself engaged in his "Audenesque" for Joseph Brodsky; "Elegy for Seamus Heaney" reflects upon the significance of how and why this particular form functions as a kind of metrical DNA for twentieth- and twenty-first-century genealogical elegy. The first three stanzas explore Heaney's repeated use of the form: firstly in "Audenesque" ("Joseph Brodsky was his friend") and then in his earlier "Elegy" for Lowell. Yet even as Matthias starts his poem by casting backward through the history of the form he also projects into the future in his first stanza, enforcing his point through the jump cut of anadiplosis,

> Seamus felt it in his feet,
> Clods of fuel in the peat.
> In the peat a fire to warm
> Children not yet even born.

These are not the contemporary "Irish Poets" of Yeats's "Under Ben Bulben" nor even the poet who will "Teach the free man how to praise" at the close of Auden's poem; rather Matthias begins by invoking an as-yet-unborn generation. This aspect of futurity pushes back productively against the retrospective nature of form in the poem. Matthias traces the form back to Blake's "The Tyger" and writes of how Auden "amend[ed]" and revised Blake's form, turning his rhetorical questions into elegiac commands. In the third stanza we read of how "Robert Lowell was shown his roots / Welcomed in an Irish town" as Matthias alludes to Lowell's visit to the Heaneys in Glanmore that is recounted in Heaney's "Elegy."

It is at the start of the fourth stanza, in the very heart of the poem, that we find "Mister Yeats" "Honored by some mortal men", but, we may note, not all. The penultimate stanza casts back yet further to Brodksy's appropriation of Auden's form in his elegy for Eliot:

> Even Possum shares the beat
> In Joseph's poem for Thomas Stearns.

> Heaney's poem for Brodsky, dead,
> Lives in turns, not Grecian urns.

It is at the very moment that Matthias describes the shared beat that he adapts it and alters Auden's aabb rhyming scheme, for, as he goes on to assert in the final line of the stanza, genealogical elegy lives on "in turns, not Grecian urns" (Matthias demonstrates this theory in practice by audaciously quadruple rhyming the lines of the final stanza). "Turns" here means both the revision and the repetition of form, a point Matthias goes on to elucidate in the final stanza:

> What dread turning plow or spade
> Having dug up things well made
> Digs now to inter a shade.
> World poets learn your trade!

In our end, as Eliot wrote in *Four Quartets,* is our beginning. Matthias concludes by turning to, and then revising, the very poem that provoked Auden to write "In Memory of W. B. Yeats": "Under Ben Bulben." Yeats's national horizon ("Irish Poets, learn your trade!") has, however, been broadened and transnationalized. Instead of the interjecting "dread voice" of Milton's "Lycidas" we find the image of the "dread turning plow or spade." The spade, of course, alludes to Heaney's manifesto poem "Digging" and Heaney himself explains the etymological significance of the plow in *Preoccupations:* "'Verse' comes from the Latin *Versus* which could mean a line of poetry but could also mean the turn that a ploughman made at the head of the field as he finished one furrow and faced back into another." Matthias's allusion to the *versus* functions like a figure of regenerative repetition in the poem, turning over the old soil to provide the elegist with the "pastures new" that the uncouth swain turns toward at the close of "Lycidas."

Yet one of the things that is repeatedly dug up even as the elegist seeks to "inter a shade" are "things well made"— that is the formal aspects of poetry—that these elegies for makers continuously revisit. This is why the first words of "Lycidas," words that herald the start of the modern elegiac era, are an admission of repetition: "Yet once more." It is the tension between *versus* (revisiting and repeating) and *poïesis* (making and revising) that drives all genealogical elegies and enables Matthias to gesture toward "children not yet even born" and importune "world poets" to learn their trade, the craft of poetry. Auden suggests at the close of his elegy for Yeats that "With the farming of a verse" we can "Make a vineyard of the curse." Elegies for poets are the point in poetry at which the returning repetition of *versus* most clearly and productively intersects with the transformative making of *poïesis* and form the "valley of making" through which Auden describes poetry flowing in his elegy for Yeats.

V.
So Large, So Friendly and So Rich: Adventures in America

"A VERY DEEP RABBIT": STRATEGIES OF EVASION AND OBLIQUITY IN SUSAN HOWE'S "THOROW"

Poetry and ambiguity are, of course, inextricably intertwined. One could go so far to say that poetry has always drawn much of its power from the force of ambiguity and that the appreciation and criticism of poetry have always relied upon the reader's capacity to embrace the moment of poetic uncertainty. This is exactly the kind of thing John Keats had in mind in his letter to his brother of 21 December 1817 when he describes "Negative Capability," "when man is capable of being in uncertainties, mysteries, doubts, without any irritable reaching after fact and reason." I would suggest that in the latter part of the twentieth century the coterie of poets that has come to be called the L=A=N=G=U=A=G=E school after Charles Bernstein's journal of the same name have sought to provoke a kind of "Positive Capability"; that is, to stimulate exactly that kind of "irritable reaching" after reason. However, this is not in order to reward the reader with the payoff of piecing sense together through the exercise *of* reason—the shoring-up of fragments that we find at the close of T. S. Eliot's *The Waste Land* or the coherence that Ezra Pound grasps toward in the final *Cantos*—rather, the "irritable reaching" is provoked in order to reveal the instability of any fact or reason that is couched in the imperfect vessel of the language that circumscribes our every thought.

As I'm sure you know, such poets have sought to reveal the gaps and discontinuities inherent in language, demonstrating through their poetry that language is not like some kind of lexical Saran wrap (or as we would have it in the UK, "cling film") that smoothly encloses, encases, and encompasses experience. Rather such poets draw our attention to the inadequacies and uncertainties of language. Their poems are often disruptive and uncomfortable to read as they draw attention to the fact that language doesn't describe the emperor's new clothes, rather that it is the emperor's new clothes. I'd like to suggest that Susan Howe yet further extends this discomfiture and tests the very limits of comprehension in her poem "Thorow" from her 1990 collection *Singularities*.

Howe's poetry has often been accused of being willfully difficult and she admits in her 1996 collection *Frame Structures* that "my early poems project aggression." Howe goes beyond authorial aggression in "Thorow" and into the realm of violence. The violence she finds embedded in the colonial history and landscape of Lake George in the Adirondacks during a writer-in-residency program becomes a violence embedded in, and enacted through, the text and our highly frustrating experience of attempting to read that text. Bernstein describes Howe in *Singularities*, "Weave[ing] at the tears in the all-too-violent fabric that imparts national identity to America. She sings of origins and hears the blanks firing in the night of her exploding syllables." Of course Bernstein undoubtedly intended the homophonic "tears" / "tears"; and he is of course right about the violence; however, I'd like to suggest that "weaving" implies a far more coherent and cohesive project that Howe ever intended. Instead it is the disjunctive, dislocated and deracinated that Howe explores in her poem. She's not knitting together the frayed edges of history in her poem but rather revealing the folly of attempting to construct *any* such coherent narrative.

The poem is a jarring exploration of the geography and conflicted history of the much contested Lake George area, which, of course, was the setting of James Fenimore Cooper's novel *The Last of the Mohicans* and was the location of the Native American massacre of British troops and their families who were surrendering to the French at Fort William Henry in 1757. The historical violence at Lake George becomes a violence enacted through language as the poem develops and becomes increasingly disintegrative. Lines and words are inverted, superimposed and scattered across the visual field of the page. This formal palimpsestic quality mimics the poem's preoccupations since it is a meditation on historical deracination, narrative disintegration and geographical disorientation. Howe recreates what she describes in her prose preface to the poem as her "panic of dislocation" in her reader as they engage with, attempt to make sense of, and try to find a way "Thorow" her poem.

From the outset of Howe's poem we are aware of words and their referents slipping from our grasp. The poem's title "Thorow" with its multiple allusions and possible meanings alerts us to the manner in which the poem will amplify and reveal the distortions in the echo chamber of history. A prose-poem section entitled "Narrative in Non-Narrative" is interposed between Howe's prose preface, which describes the circumstances of her sojourn at Lake George, and the poetic meat of the poem, which gestures toward the significance of her title. The word "Thorow" is, we learn, an allusion to Sir Humfrey Gilbert's work *A Discourse of a Discovery for a New Passage to Cataia* in which he aims, "To prove that the Indians aforenamed came not by the Northeast, and that there is no thorow passage navigable that way." Thus, the title of the poem in the first instance is taken from the idea of finding one's way through, of traversing territory (and I'll come back to that idea of "traversing" later).

The second echo, of course, is of the name of the writer Henry David Thoreau, and of his autobiographical work set upon another New England lake, *Walden*. However, in "Narrative in Non-Narrative" Howe takes pains to point out that "Thoreau never visited the Adirondacks." Within the body of the poem we find a third meaning of the word in the intention to "thorow out all / The Five Nations" (this was the name for the five tribes that made up the Iroquois league). Thus the heterographic and homophonic ambiguity embedded in the title which can be read as (and bear with me)—to throw / to find a way through / and the writer Thoreau—thorows down the authorial gauntlet. As Lyn Hejinian points out in *The Language of Inquiry,* "It is the difference between rod and red and rid that makes them mean. Wordplay, in this sense, foregrounds the relationships between words." Howe takes this further. Her fascination with and focus on paronomasia and orthography in the poem foregrounds the gaps and holes in the ostensibly coherent surfaces of both history and the language that we use to convey it.

As Jenny White argues in "The Landscape of Susan Howe's 'Thorow'": "Naming and claiming go hand in hand, and the poem repeatedly mentions borders, divisions, and property markers. These borders are both insisted on and broken down, for example in the lines, 'Fence blown down in a winter storm / darkened by outstripped possession / Field stretching out of the world.'" And as Howe herself points out in *The Birth-mark: Unsettling the wilderness in American literary history*, "I am trying to understand what went wrong when the first Europeans stepped on shore here. They came for some reason, something pushed them. What pushed them? Isn't it bitterly ironic that many of them were fleeing the devastation caused by enclosure laws back in Britain and the first thing they did here was to put up fences?" I'd like to take White's excellent point about the broken boundaries a step further and suggest that Howe is also doing this with form and language in the poem. She's breaking down the barriers between words. She is, as she says in her poem, "Author the real author / acting the part of a scout." She's leading us, however, not into Charles Olsen's field of composition, a wide-open space of possibility and American expansiveness, but rather down a rabbit hole of confusion, spelunking in the cave of making, and I'd like you to follow me following her now.

In an interview with Lynn Keller Howe explained her decision to mirror and invert the text on pages 56 and 57 of *Singularities* which face each other: "with 'Thorow' I had done one scattered page and made a Xerox copy and suddenly there were two lying on my desk beside each other, and it seemed to me the scattering effect was stronger if I repeated them so the image would travel across facing pages. The pages reflected and strengthened each other." But what is reflected and how accurately; and what, exactly is strengthened here? I think one of the best ways to get a sense of this is to listen to Howe reading this section of her poem. (One may find recordings on the marvelous PennSound website.)

It was on hearing Howe read her own work that I noted the verbal though not textual repetition of "Gabion / Parapet" in her performance of page 56. This phrase becomes a hinge in the poem, a fulcrum upon which possible meaning may turn. Again, Howe brings us to the violently broken boundary, the line of defense at

Fort William Henry, the British garrison besieged by the French. This incident is clearly alluded to in the lines "Parted with the Otterware / at the three Rivers, / & are / Gone to have a Treaty / with the French at Oswego / & singing their war song / The French Hatchet Messages." Though the French "Plenipo" (a shortening of plenipotentiary) was invested with full power to negotiate terms with the British, the word "hatchet"—the weapon of choice of the tribes of the "Five Nations"—is ominous since the French had hired native American mercenaries. It was this contingent of the French army that massacred the surrendering British troops. Here we find the English and French word for military fortifications abutting each other, like the armies facing off at the siege. A *gabion* is an incarnation of the sandbag, a cylindrical woven wicker container, open at each end, to be filled with dirt. The "Gabion" comes under attack in the lines "Traverse canon night siege Constant firing" that shatters the "Tranquility of a garrison." Again, with this image of the broken gabion, the shattered vessel, I think we find Howe exploring ideas of language and containment, language under siege, broken and bleeding on this page. We find other kinds of broken and deracinated symbols on the page too; the chips, arrowheads, coins, and hieroglyphs that are capable of being communicatory currency but also unreadable without the Rosetta stone of context.

And what of what is *not* reflected in the mirror image in the distorted Rorschach of pages 56 and 57? Well, most obviously the moment of authorial exasperation that starts section 3 on page 56, an exasperation enforced by Howe's own reading of the poem "Cannot be / every / where I entreat / snapt / resolution." What is "snapped" here is not just the resolution of the siege at Fort William Henry and the broken treaty, but also any possible resolution of the poem. The betrayal of the expectation of understanding. This irresolution is typographically underscored by the inversion and disruption of "resolution." It is the first inverted word of the poem and the most typographically distorted word within "Thorow." It is at this point that the poem snaps, a plank in reason breaks, and we fall with Howe into the rabbit hole, where the troubled waters of Lake George reflect back a distorted image of the Lake's history and signifiers do *not* reflect what is intended to be signified.

An example of this distorted reflection is apparent in the inverted narrative of the negotiation of the peace. Here we read of how "the far nations / over the lakes / Messengers say / The War Belt / & singing their war song / The French Hatchet / Messages." This is the other side's story as is made apparent in the missing and distorted word from page 56 "covery" which operates on a number of possible levels. Most obviously this is a "snapt" word, the "disc" a few lines above divorced from the "covery" of its closure, thus the word discovery requires recovery. I was also intrigued to read Ian Kenneth Steele's 1990 account of the siege, *Fort William Henry and the Massacre;* and, in particular, I found mention of a British soldier, one Wells Coverly (of course, Howe omits the "l" and typographically disrupts the proper name) who was taken prisoner and held for many months by the French. Perhaps this "covery" embodies poor Wells (his first name suggesting that very deep rabbit hole too). The fact that page 57 represents the ostensible victor's side is also typographically apparent in the upstanding and non-inverted "Parapet" and the line "Traverse canon night siege Constant firing" is one-sided (their side) and the right way up.

But what of the baffling heart of these two passages, which appears inverted on page 56 and right-way-up on page 57? The insistent printing instructions that disintegrate into ungrammatical nonsense:

> Frames should be exactly
> fitted to the paper, the Margins
> of which will not per [mit]
> a very deep Rabbit

The Rabbit embeds both the practical and the whimsical here, suggesting not only the indentation of the carpenter's rabbet but also the chthonic rabbit hole.

We have come across the Rabbit's path earlier in the poem when we read of the writer "Scribbling the ineffable / See only the tracks of rabbit" (47). Here Howe, the white rabbit, is trying not to scribble the ineffable, to write the indescribable; rather she is trying to sound its depth, to plumb the profundity of what happened at Lake George, but not in order to explain it. Rather she reveals how imperfect the language we have to attempt to convey such history is, through the etymological slippage that we find in the muscular two-syllable verbs of negotiation and diplomacy used in this passage: "entreat" "permit," and, for Howe's purposes, the most important: "traverse." This slipperiness is underscored by the square brackets applied to "per [mit]" which breaks it down into its original components, "*per*" of course from the Latin "through" (and we're back to "thorow") and "*mittere*," to send. The importunate "entreat" suggests its old French root "*traiter*" (treat) and, of course, shades of treachery; and finally, as I mentioned earlier, I'd like to direct your attention to "traverse."

Like one of her great poetic heroes, Charles Olson, Howe loves words that embed the very idea of poetry, and here we find the repeated use of the word and idea of "traverse" in a poem in three parts. Traverse of course means to cross and here it seems to refer to many kinds of crossings and conveyance: crossing boundaries topographically and typographically, crossing Lake George, and most significantly, attempting to convey meaning through language, and the ultimate failure of that attempted crossing. In Latin, *transversere* also means to "throw" across, and so we come back to Howe's title and her preface where modern-day Lake George is described as "a travesty." Howe's poem enacts the impossibility of traversing—conveying—a travesty. She describes this in her prose-poem section "Narrative non-Narrative" thus, "Work penetrated by the edge of author traverses multiplicities, light letters exploding apprehension suppose when individual hearing." She discomforts and challenges her reader the "individual hearing" in "Thorow" as she explodes apprehension until we become apprehensive. In this way she reveals not only the betrayal that occurred at Fort William in 1757 but also the way in which language always betrays us. We are become Alice chasing after Howe's white rabbit and language is revealed as being as stable and solid as the grin on a Cheshire cat.

THE POETRY OF 9/11: KEEPING YES AND NO UNSPLIT IN THE DIALECTIC OF DISASTER

9/11 was an event that simultaneously demands and defies description. The subsequent conflicts in Iraq and Afghanistan, have, of course, generated war poetry (such as Brian Turner's collection *Here, Bullet*) and antiwar poetry such as may be found in Sam Hamill's anthology *Poets Against the War,* but for the purposes of this essay I am particularly interested in verse that focuses on the initial attack rather than the ongoing conflict. I am especially keen to explore why and how what happened that day presents a highly problematic challenge to attempts at verse representation.

In the years since the attacks there have been many efforts in various forms and genres to explore the events of that day and attempts to commemorate the loss of three thousand lives. Documentaries such as Henry Singer's *The Falling Man;* films like the British director Paul Greengrass's *United 93;* novels (among the most notable Jonathan Safran Foer's *Extremely Loud and Incredibly Close* and Don DeLillo's *Falling Man*); and graphic novels, for example Art Spiegelman's *In The Shadow of No Towers.* Though all of these genres struggle in various ways to encompass and examine the atrocity I would like to suggest that what happened poses a very difficult and distinct problem for the poet, and that poetic language and forms face a particularly difficult challenge under the pressure of grappling with such an unthinkable atrocity.

Unlike the other forms I've already mentioned—film, documentary, fiction and graphic novel—poetry is fundamentally a metaphoric and metonymic form of art, and it's this reliance on imaginative substitutions that has proved to be the hardest challenge that the poets who write about 9/11 have faced. For example, in her poem "How to Write a Poem After September 11th," which can be found in a 2002 anthology of New York poets titled *Poetry After 9-11,* Nikki Moustaki warns other poets against the already trite and tired metaphors of the event ("Don't compare the planes to birds. Please. / Don't call the windows eyes"). Indeed, as Robert Pinsky points out in his poem "9/11" one of the greatest challenges poets face is how horrifically visual an event the attacks were, a fact that often seems to undermine attempts at poetic imagery:

> We adore images, we like the spectacle
> Of speed and size, the working of prodigious
> Systems. So on television we watched
>
> The terrible spectacle, repetitiously gazing
> Until we were sick not only of the sight
> Of our prodigious systems turned against us
>
> But of the very systems of our watching.
> The date became a word, an anniversary
> That we inscribed with meanings—

The event becomes its own metaphor, its own shorthand for the unthinkable. In this the poets of 9/11 share many of the same challenges that face the poets of the AIDS epidemic which, as Mark Doty explains in his poem "Atlantis," is "not even a real word / but an acronym, a vacant / four-letter cipher // that draws meanings into itself, / reconstitutes the world." 9/11 is in many ways an imaginative black hole, an event so atrocious that it centripetally sucks the significance out of any metaphor that attempts to bridge and broach the representational gap. In the days immediately after the fall of the twin World Trade Center towers, journalists drew on the language of a previous unthinkable and horrifying loss of life—the atomic attacks on Hiroshima and Nagasaki—to provide them with a metaphor of what was left: "ground zero," a phrase which almost immediately became what Orwell would have described as a "dying metaphor," a cliché before the event had even started to be assimilated into our collective cultural consciousness.

Though Theodor Adorno famously asserted that "to write lyric poetry after Auschwitz is barbaric." I am far more inclined to agree with the Holocaust poet Paul Celan when he suggests in his poem "*Sprich auch du,*" ("Speak, you also"):

> Speak—
> But keep yes and no unsplit.
> And give your say this meaning:
> give it the shade.

The best poems to address 9/11 (and of course I realize that's a very subjective standard) seem to do exactly this. Indeed, I shall go on to suggest that not the best poetry, but also the best prose about 9/11, such as Foer's *Extremely Loud and Incredibly Close*, manages to avoid splitting yes and no, and resists closure. These works avoid the temptingly divisive polarities of the myths of them and us, before and after, good and bad, that the human mind often finds solace in to when confronted with unthinkable horrors. This dangerous temptation of dichotomization, the dialectic of them and us, is considered in Karen Swenson's poem "We," "One pronoun keeps at bay our guilt / they they they they they they."

Though I'd argue that poetry is probably the genre most compromised in its efforts to represent 9/11 due to the utterly unambiguous nature of the catastrophe, it seems to be the genre that we most frequently sought recourse to in the days, months and years after the event. Many looked to a poem published sixty-two years previously, W. H. Auden's poem composed on the brink of the Second World War, "September 1, 1939." Auden's poem was widely circulated in email as a consolatory response to the attacks and featured on the pages of several newspapers both here and abroad. (Stephanie Burt has published a very good article in *American Literary History* titled "'September 1, 1939' Revisited" about the subsequent dissemination of the poem). The poem displays not only uncannily prescient lines such as "The unmentionable odour of death / Offends the September night" and "blind skyscrapers use / Their full height to proclaim / The strength of Collective Man" but also suggests that the role of the poet is to "show an affirming flame" and instructs us to "love one another or die." However, it is worth remembering that it was that very line that caused Auden eventually to disown the poem due to its "incurable dishonesty." Yet as Burt points out in her article,

"The virtues that the poem exhibited in 1939 are inseparable from the poem's renewed appeal in 2001; they are also inseparable from the reasons Auden disowned it." The poem's appeal to a shell-shocked readership in 2001 lies in the very weakness that Auden came to despise: it distorts and simplifies, comfortingly overstating the poet's powers to heal and offering us soothingly trite, and ultimately hollow, consolation: an affirming "yes."

Though Auden's poem offered in many ways a reassuringly temporally remote lens through which to look at the events of 9/11 there are also, of course, thousands of contemporary poems that responded directly to the attacks. I'd like to focus on Wislawa Szymborska's 2005 poem "Photograph from September 11." It was first published in her collection *Monologue of a Dog Ensnared in History*, and was selected by the artist Jenny Holzer to feature alongside several other poems for an installation of slowly scrolling text that would be on display in the rebuilt World Trade Center Seven. However, the owners of World Trade Center Seven, Larry and Clara Silverstein, found the poem to be distasteful and requested that the poem be excluded from the installation. One may find a series of fascinating essays by critics such as Jahan Ramanzani and poets such as Mark Doty that debate the wisdom of this choice and the nature of public acts of commemoration on the Poetry Foundation's website. I quote from James Tatum's essay: "the Silversteins were distressed by its focus on the plummeting bodies of those who 'jumped from the burning floors, down / —one, two, a few more, / higher, lower.'" Yet as Tatum argues:

> "Photograph from September 11" shows a wisdom in poetry that no public memorial anywhere can ever hope to equal, because every memorial and monument that is built aims to be a final word about what it commemorates. This is why "closure" and words like it have such a hollow ring to them. Poetry like "Photograph from September 11" is where a poetics of griefs public or private can be found, if they are to be found anywhere.

Indeed it's this very closure, offered by Auden in advance of the events of the Second World War, that mortally undermines his poem. I'd like now to explore this resistance, this attempt, as Celan has it, "to keep yes and no unsplit" in Szymborska's poem.

"Photograph from 9/11" and "September 1, 1939" both share similar compositional agendas and concerns. Both poems focus on a precise moment in time, a moment when the world is on the brink and about to be irreversibly altered. Both poems explore the importance and responsibilities of the individual, and in particular the role of the poet in society. Both poems are written from the perspective of poets from outside America. And both poems have been censored, Auden's poem by the poet himself and Szymborska's by the owners of the rebuilt World Trade Center Seven. However, as we shall see, the poems fundamentally diverge on the matter of the resistance of closure.

Whereas Auden locates himself in a particular time, the evening of 1ˢᵗ September 1939, and place, "one of the dives / On Fifty-second Street," at the outset of his poem, Szymborska focuses instead on a photograph of a particular time and place, one of the horrifying photographs of people jumping from the Trade Centers, preferring to exert one final, terrifying and, to anyone not in their awful position, unthinkable act of control of their fates, rather than to succumb to the smoke and flames within the towers. We read in the second stanza of how:

> The photograph halted them in life,
> and now keeps them
> above the earth toward the earth.

The photograph and then, in turn, Szymborska's ekphrastic poem about the photograph freeze the fallen right on the boundary, the liminal moment in the dialectic of disaster between alive and dead; before and after. Indeed Szymborska's tercets formally recreate this moment, each an endstopped snapshot of the descent, yet the three-line form resists the clicking closure of the couplet or the certainty of the quatrain. The only time in the poem that Szymborska uses the quatrain, in the fourth stanza, it is in order to mimetically recreate the unfurling fall.

Szymborska manages carefully to balance between the polarities of the private and public, and the interior and exterior, in the third stanza, where we read of how:

> Each is still complete,
> with a particular face
> and blood well hidden.

She tenderly preserves their individual identities, their "particular faces" while also protecting their identities. "Blood well hidden" emphatically gestures toward their unavoidable fates, and yet also retains the semblance of privacy at this moment which was to become one of the most public of the modern era.

The poem wears its richly symbolic imagery lightly, and it would be easy to miss the significance of the keys and coins that fall from the falling in the fourth stanza. Coins unavoidably suggest the free market economics that Osama bin Laden sought to attack in his strikes on the Trade Centers. Let us not forget he'd already previously attempted to bring down these symbols of American economic success in a 1992 bombing attempt. Keys have always been richly suggestive of the liminal, of the boundary between two states. Indeed, we may find exactly this idea in *Extremely Loud and Incredibly Close*, Foer's novel about a boy, Oskar Schell, whose father is killed at the World Trade Center. While searching through his father's possessions Oskar happens upon a key labeled with the name "Black." The novel follows him on his quest to find the lock that corresponds to this key, a quest that he believes will bring him closer to his father. The novel, like Szymborska's poem, hangs in the balance as it resists the dialectic of disaster, the tempting yet reductive modes of oppositional thinking that we often use to make senses of catastrophe and atrocity. Oskar's story seems to be built around many such oppositional structures and Oskar's quest takes the form of attempting to heal this rift.

He is a boy who only wears white who is searching for a person by the name of Black, he is obsessed with presence and absence (and in particular the absence of his father's body); his grandparents live in an apartment zoned into "nothing" and "something" spaces; his grandfather, a mute, has Yes and No tattooed upon his hands, so when he rubs his hands together or claps he joins yes with no. Oskar compulsively searches for images of bodies frozen in their fall from the towers, scrutinizing each in the hope of finding out what may have happened to his father. Most importantly, Oskar and his creator Foer resist closure in the final pages of the novel by creating a flipbook of a series of images of one of the people falling from the towers. Rather than charting this individual's inexorable descent Oskar arranges the images in reverse, creating the illusion of the individual floating back up into what Szymborska calls "the realm of the air" restoring them to possibility rather than finality.

Szymborska does this while remaining in the realm of the linguistic rather than visual at the close of her poem and we read of how the falling are:

> ... still within the air's reach,
> within the compass of places
> that have just now opened.
>
> I can do only two things for them—
> describe this flight
> and not add a last line.

Whereas in Auden's poem the skyscrapers reach into the air, here the air's reach almost seems to cradle the falling in this moment in which the world has been irrevocably altered forever. This new vista, "the compass of places / that have just now opened," of course applies in some way to all us, and not just those souls who sought to exercise, in the final moments of their lives, the choice the hijacker's murderous acts afforded them.

Szymborska turns in her final stanza to consider the problem of written representation of disasters. Even if we do add "a last line," such events always seem to resist any attempts at linguistic closure. When teaching a course about representations of disaster I was struck by how many writers seek to revisit and add to their accounts of catastrophe. For example, in 1985 John Hersey adds a whole chapter entitled

"Aftermath" to his Pulitzer-prize-winning 1946 book *Hiroshima,* while in 2000 Haruki Murakami added a philosophical treatise and the biographies of several members of the AUM cult to *Underground,* his 1997 account of the Sarin gas attacks on the Tokyo subway. In bearing witness ("describing this flight") yet refusing closure ("not adding a last line") Szymborska reconsiders the role of the writer when confronted with catastrophe. Rather than showing an "affirming" yea-saying flame as Auden suggested in 1939, Szymborska resists the temptations of yes and no, before and after, keeping them unsplit as Celan invites us to. She gives her words shade, and in the shade her poem simultaneously exercises enormous restraint and power.

THE OFFSPRING OF EZRA POUND'S PACT?
MARK DOTY'S "LETTER TO WALT WHITMAN"

In his 1916 poem "a Pact," Ezra Pound admits to having "detested" Walt Whitman "long enough." He grudgingly admits, "It was you that broke the new wood," yet regards Whitman's work to be unfinished, arguing that, "Now is a time for carving." The poem concludes with a half-hearted attempt at reconciliation: "We have one sap and one root—Let there be commerce between us."

In this essay I'd like to consider the monumental shadow cast by the shade of Whitman on Mark Doty and his recent "Letter to Walt Whitman," examine the figuration of the dead poet in relation to the living, and establish the nature of the "commerce" between them. Is Whitman an unassailable or an approachable poetic icon? How are issues of influence dealt with? To what extent does this poem crystallize the process of poetic inheritance? Does Doty seek to appease the figure of Whitman or is the dynamic far more competitive? Could Doty be regarded as the offspring of Pound's "Pact"? And, is it true, as Doty asserts, that Whitman "wrote the book against which we are read'?

In "Song of Myself," from his 1855 collection *Leaves of Grass*, Whitman informs us, "He most honors my style who learns under it to destroy the teacher." Many subsequent poets have viewed this as an invitation. Whitman's style could itself be defined as a shattering of the forms of *his* teachers, a feat which, in turn, made his free-verse, long-lined and oratorical style a catalytic and pervasive mode for those poets who've followed him. Whitman's successors frequently seem willfully to misread his challenge by transposing the incitement to destroy from Whitman's style to the man and his beliefs. Let it be noted that the line implies that Whitman himself is not the teacher, but rather that his style is the instructor to be overcome. Whitman correctly foresaw that his style would become so unavoidable as to require some act of usurpation on the part of succeeding generations of poets. Thus, by the very process of razing Whitman's poetic influence, his successor tacitly bestows the honor of unavoidability upon his poetic style.

Whitman's apparent arrogance was to be proved entirely justified, and in his 1860 poem "Poets to Come" he even foresaw *this*, as he hectoringly addressed "a new brood, native, athletic, continental, greater than before known, / Arouse! for you must justify me." In hindsight, Whitman's expectations do not seem immodest, and are tempered by a realistic assessment of his own importance. Whitman doesn't overestimate his own poetic worth. Rather, he recognizes that, "I myself but write one or two indicative words for the future, / I but advance a moment only to wheel and hurry back I the darkness." This is a beneficent, rather than provocative, appeal to his successors. Unlike many poets who seem profoundly concerned with how their poetic reputations will fare after their deaths, Whitman generously surrenders up his legacy to the mercies of coming generations of poets. It's up to them, as Whitman put it, to "prove and define it." Whitman knows that his time will pass and is now "Expecting the main thing from you."

Mark Doty's expansive and discursive "Letter to Walt Whitman," published in his 2001 collection *Source*, begins by inverting the weight of expectation that Whitman had placed on his inheritors. Doty hesitatingly embarks on his apostrophic address in the knowledge that, "you've been bothered // all century, poets lining up / to claim lineage." The very act of writing such a poem, addressed to the shade of an illustrious forebear, is, after all, a means of claiming direct descent. However, Doty treads with care. Unlike Pound, who posits a close, conflicted, and paternalistic relationship in "A Pact"—"I come to you as a grown child / who has had a pig-headed father"—Doty regards Whitman as a distant and avuncular figure, commenting rather than lamenting that: " I am so far from you, Uncle." Thus Doty neatly sidesteps the issue of the competitive and Oedipal inheritance anxiety with which a critic such as Harold Bloom might expect such a poem to be fraught. Doty has executed a poetic maneuver akin to a knight move in chess by imaging himself as Whitman's nephew, an oblique relationship with no direct line of inheritance.

These first few stanzas do not, however, ignore Whitman's comments regarding the necessity of overcoming one's teachers, and Doty deftly contends with this potentially problematic issue. The seemingly contradictory nature of Whitman, as made apparent in his instruction to shatter his style in order to do it honor, is encapsulated in the lines describing "our prophet / who enjoins us to follow / —what else?—our own lights." Doty is following *his* own lights by conflating formal adherence to regular unrhymed quatrains with Whitman's own poetic inclination toward the digressive and discursive. The continued enjambment (often across stanza breaks) and frequent caesurae highlight the manner in which form has been superimposed upon a poetic mode akin to Whitman's. Thus Doty appears to overcome Whitman's style even as he incorporates it into his poem, as the Whitmanesque inclination toward long-lined prolixity struggles against the bounds of stanzaic confinement. Doty also usurps Whitman's style by looking beyond poetry as a means of addressing the dead poet. Instead, he details modes of address far more accessible and democratic than poetry, such as a glossy coffee table book, described by Doty as "a twentieth-century // letter to you," where passages from Whitman are juxtaposed with tasteful photographs celebrating the male form. Doty sees yet another kind of letter to Whitman in the democratic scripture of graffiti, "… the scrawls / beneath the underpass, ruby and golden / cuneiform reinscribed on train-car sides."

We now read of a pilgrimage that Doty made to Whitman's house in low-rent and run-down Camden, New Jersey, which proves to be a latter-day *locus amoenus* for one of the first poets of the urban experience. Doty deploys Whitman's "catalogue technique" in order to enumerate those possessions of the dead poet on display around the house: "Here your backpack, crumpled like a leather // sigh, a bit of your handwriting, framed; / a menu for a testimonial, and far too many // photos of your tomb." The qualification "far too many" is telling. Doty seems to imply that the impulse to monumentalize Whitman is excessive and distancing. In his 1981 book *The Life of the Poet*, on the beginning and ending of poetic careers, Lawrence

Lipking is much concerned with the manner in which poets are commemorated, particularly in poems occasioned by their deaths. He calls these poems "*tombeaux,*" after Mallarme's poems on the deaths of Edgar Allan Poe, Charles Baudelaire, Theophile Gautier and Paul Verlaine, and argues that: "Poets may try to design their own memorials, but all they can be sure of is the body of their work; the monument, the way the work will be remembered, must be left to other hands. Very quickly the poet ceases to control his fate." As Doty points out, Whitman had been complicit in this "useless poem" and had designed his own tomb in Harleigh cemetery, Camden. However, the tomb of which Lipking writes is not the place where the dead poet's body is interred, but rather the manner in which their poetic reputation is enshrined. Though Whitman had exerted control over the design of his actual tomb, he was happy, in poems such as "Poets to Come," to commend his poetic reputation to coming generations of poets. Thus, the photographs of Whitman's tomb are not only excessive but also, in some ways, inappropriate. Whitman had attempted in verse to prevent just such a response to his legacy, and he appreciated that the dead poet lives on in what other poets choose to take from him rather than in what he wills to them.

Rather than focusing on the images of Whitman's deadening tomb, Doty's eye alights upon "one thing [that] made you seem alive: // your parrot, Walt, friend of the last years." This instantly brought to mind Julian Barnes's brilliant exposition upon and in *Flaubert's Parrot.* Yet it becomes apparent that this is less a case of "Walt Whitman, *c'est moi*" and more "Walt Whitman *est le perroquet.*" Doty describes the jaunty stuffed bird with his "head crooked toward the future." This fits with Whitman's own description of himself glancing toward his successor in "Poets to Come": "I am a man who, sauntering along without fully stopping, turns a / casual look upon you and then averts his face." The parrot could also be seen to symbolize a misguided mode of learning from Whitman, literally parrot-fashion:

> I thought if I leaned near that glass I bent,
> patriarch, closer to you—he had

> your ear, didn't he, and if I leaned
> toward his still-inquiring, precious eye ...

Note that Doty has inverted the anticipated exchange of information. Whitman talks to the parrot, rather than, as might be expected, the parrot reciting Whitman's own words back at him.

The reincarnatory power of Whitman's parrot affords Doty the luxury of proximity and enables him to question the patriarch of American poetry as he asks "Did you mean it?" Under the aegis of "it" Doty seems to address the two cornerstones of belief that Whitman repeatedly touched on in his poetry: the ideal of a democratic utopia and Whitman's pet concept of "adhesiveness." However, Whitman doesn't have a chance to respond, since Doty is now interrupted, roused from his poetic reverie not by a person from Porlock, but rather by "two Jehovah's Witnesses." Doty's response to this unwanted intrusion enables him obliquely to illustrate a fundamental change which poets have undergone since Whitman's day:

> ... Our poets fear
> the didactic, the sweeping claim; we let
> the televangelists and door-to-door
> preachers talk hope and apocalypse
>
> while we tend more private gardens.

The interruption enables Doty to compare poetry past with poetry present without directly criticizing Whitman's sweeping claims nor denigrating his hopes. Rather, the contrast affords Doty the opportunity to place Whitman's life and achievement in the contest of his era. Doty admits to being awe-struck. "It stops / my breath, to think of what you said," and wonders "how" Whitman did it. Whitman responds to Doty's questions "as the dead do." Which is, of course, not at all.

Doty now describes his itinerant existence as a "visiting poet" on a book tour in Ohio, incarcerated in a hotel room "bland as a tomb." The simile enforces the very blandness not only of Doty's hotel room but also of Whitman's actual tomb. Doty's "Letter" is, in many ways, a far more fitting tribute to the dead poet as it interrogates and reanimates his legacy. Instead of Doty getting a response from Whitman and seeing the world from his perspective, Whitman is invited to see the world through Doty's eyes "I'd like you to see my view." Yet what Doty *sees* is directly informed by the dead poet's vision. The sight of the scurrying Ohioians many stories below, "black sparks from an original flame," prompts Doty to allude to Whitman's poem, "There Was a Child Went Forth," where the poet enquires "Whether that which appears so is, or is it all flashes and specks? / Men and women crowding fast in the streets, if they are not flashes and specks what are they?" Doty's figuration of Whitman as an "original flame," both originating and innovative, may also suggest Dante's encounter with Arnaut Daniel in Purgatory, where the Provençal troubadour is consumed by a purifying flame in order to do penance for his earthly promiscuity. The encounter is best remembered for the tag bestowed upon Daniel: "*il miglior fabbro*" ('the better craftsman'). Could this, therefore be a nod on Doty's part to Whitman's superiority? This was, of course, also the phrase with which T. S. Eliot chose to dedicate *The Waste Land* to Ezra Pound, so could we also regard Doty's description of Whitman's "original flame" as a subtle gesture toward Pound and his Pact?

This possible reading is enforced by another Dantean allusion a few stanzas further on: "Of our company in your century, / dust and silence almost all erase." Doty, who shares a common sexuality as well as vocation with Whitman, alludes to the lot of nineteenth-century homosexuals in a manner reminiscent to that which Dante used to describe the lot of thirteenth- and early-fourteenth-century homosexuals in the *Inferno*. The Dante *personaggio* encounters the charred figures of his old mentor Brunetto Latini and his "*masnada*" (a company or gang) on the burning sands of the seventh circle of hell. Latini and his company were damned due to what, in the theological hierarchy of the time, was regarded as violence against nature. Yet Dante perceives Latini's tragic flaw not to be *his* sexuality but rather this obsession with his own posthumous renown. No such criticism could be leveled at Whitman, and Doty muses on what

Whitman might have made of "the grassy persistence / of your name." Unlike Latini, Doty fears that Whitman would find his eponymous persistence cheapening, a mere shorthand for cultural authority:

> ... I've crossed the Walt Whitman Bridge
>
> PA to Jersey, past Walt Whitman High,
> even stopped on the Turnpike at
> (denigration of our brightest hopes)
> the Walt Whitman Service Area.

Whitman's dream of democracy has been soured by Capitalism and his name has been appropriated for its purposes. The "omnistore" has taken the place of Whitman's omnific aspirations. For, as Doty explains, poems "are written on the back of time, / inscriptions on the wrong side of a photograph: / scribbled flourish of our possibility." The broader cultural possibilities and hopes inscribed in Whitman's verse on the back of the nineteenth-century have not come to fruition.

Doty draws another poet into the equation as he asks: Is it true then, what your descendant said, / that poetry makes nothing happen?" This indirect interrogation is, of course, a quotation taken from W. H. Auden's elegy "In Memory of W. B. Yeats." Doty answers his own question even as he poses it. In figuring Auden as Whitman's descendant (and, in turn, himself as a descendant of them both) Doty implies that poetry *inevitably* makes something happen by the way it influences succeeding generations of poets. Though the social possibilities described in Whitman's verse haven't come to fruition, the flourish of the possibility made apparent in his verse *has*. What Whitman's poetry makes happen is the inevitable comparisons to, and inescapable influence of, his work. As Doty puts it: "You wrote the book against which we are read."

Yet by "we" Doty seems to mean not only contemporary poets but also latter-day Americans, those who consume "As if to purchase were to celebrate." Doty manages partially to reconcile the acquisitive present to Whitman's vision by recasting consumerism in Whitman's image. Drawing on a quote from Whitman's poem "The Sleepers,"

Doty substitutes the modern activity of shopping for the sleep that Whitman imagines as a unifying force. In shopping, as in sleeping, Doty finds an unavoidable equality of activity.

In hindsight Whitman's hopes could be considered naïve, for, as Doty asks: "... Who could be hopeful // for the sheer ascending numbers of us, / the poisoned sky and trees?" Yet again Whitman responds "as the dead do." This phrase not only functions as an elegiac refrain for the purposes of Doty's "Letter" but also reinforces the fact that this is the underlying refrain of all poems that address the dead. The dead can't and don't answer the questions put to them in such poems, but the very act of writing the poem seems to provide and answer in itself. Thus, the aim of Doty's poem seems not to be elegiac consolation, but rather poetic clarification.

The poem concludes "in the parking lot waiting for you." Yet Doty is not waiting for an answer from Whitman, but rather following his example. At the end of "Song of Myself," Whitman bequeaths himself not to his poetic inheritors and the "grassy persistence" of posthumous acclaim, but rather to the earth and the "grass [he] loves." He instructs those that seek him to "look for me under your boot-soles.": "Failing to fetch me at first keep encouraged, / Missing me one place search another, / I stop somewhere waiting for you." Unlike Pound, who forcibly conflates Whitman with himself in the final word of his "Pact"—"us"—Doty's last word, like Whitman's at the close of "Poets to Come" and "Song of Myself," unselfishly addresses another, "you." Doty communes with Whitman, whereas Pound proposes commerce. Rather than detesting Whitman, Doty imagines an avuncular and approachable figure, and does not make the mistake of confusing the life with the work. That is not to say that Doty does not criticize Whitman the man, but when he does so, he is both reasonable and respectful. Doty both formally celebrates and censures Whitman's style by incorporating and overcoming it, and, in doing so, does him the honor of unavoidablity. Doty, unlike Pound, has no ambition to carve up Whitman's legacy. Rather than working through any kind of anxiety of influence, Doty's "Letter" seems happy to reveal the acquisition of influence, in the process demonstrating *how* Whitman's poetry "makes something happen" in the manner in which it influences succeeding generations of poets. Whitman functions as muse as well as master to Doty, and his enduring legacy, the right to sing a song of oneself, lives on in the poem that Doty addresses to him.

Acknowledgments

I wish to thank Robert Archambeau for suggesting I write this collection of essays and Marc Vincenz at the MadHat Press for making it possible. I would also like to thank F. J. Bergmann for her diligent copyediting and for alerting me to the American carpenter's "rabbet" which I was unfamiliar with.

This book is a collaborative effort. I have benefited hugely from the conversations that I've had over the years with many of my colleagues at the University of Houston and beyond, particularly Jen Wingard, Lynn Voskuil, Ann Christensen, Sarah Ehlers, Robert Cremins, Greg Garrard, John Matthias, Charles O. Hartman, David Mikics, Mark Scroggins, John Mole, Mark Ford, Greg Delanty, and Stephanie Burt. I owe John Sutherland for many things and am indebted to him for putting me in touch with Karl Miller before Karl's death in 2014. I am extremely grateful to Karl's widow Jane for allowing me to reproduce my conversation with her husband here and to Karl's sons for their input on the interview. I am also very thankful to Clive Wilmer and August Kleinzahler for their continued help with all things Gunn-related.

I would like to thank Nick Tubby for the information about his fascinating forebears, Mrs. Biddy Hodge and Frank Mozart Walker. I would also like to thank Gustavo Turner for suggesting the Zbigniew Herbert entry in my A–Z of Seamus Heaney. I'm particularly grateful to Brian Rogers for looking after me as the project coalesced during my period of convalescence due to a broken foot over the summer of 2017. Lisa Hilton, Sara Burningham, Russell Cotton, Eric Sandler continue to inspire and delight. I owe a special thanks to my cousin Dennis Hayes and his wife Brenda for being Madre and Papa to my kids during the final stages of writing this book and to Annie and Amanda Crane for being amazing American aunties to Seamus and Elizabeth.

This is book is dedicated to the extraordinary Jordan J. Evans, who was with me on the most important transatlantic trip of my life in May 2005. Thank you.

A version of "Two Genealogical Elegies for Seamus Heaney," was previously published in *Literary Imagination* (Oxford University Press), Volume 18, Issue 3: 1–9.

A version of "'Breaking Bread with the Dead': W. H. Auden, Seamus Heaney and Yeats's legacy" (Book Chapter) appears in *Yeats Annual* 17 (Palgrave Macmillan, Spring 2008): 197–226.

Both articles, which in their original form provide full citation details that are omitted here, are reproduced with kind permission.

About the Author

SALLY CONNOLLY was born in the UK during the uncharacteristically scorching hot summer of 1976. This early discomfort spawned a life-long hatred of the sun, and consequently, she is rather disgruntled to find herself living in Houston even though the food there is excellent. She worked as a miner, artist's model, literary agent and barmaid before settling on poetry critic as a life-long vocation. Her brother Peter currently holds the world record for skateboarding downhill at 91.17 mph.

Apart from a very brief flirtation with the law (as a practitioner rather than, as was family tradition, a criminal) she has expended almost all of her academic efforts on poetry. After spending several years studying at University College London she was finally prised out her glorious Bloomsbury existence by the lure of a Kennedy Scholarship at Harvard University. As a Visiting Fellow at Harvard she spent almost every waking hour either wallowing in the Robert Lowell archive at the Houghton Library or being led astray by the dedicatee of this book. She is very proud that she managed to infiltrate the Signet Society during her time there. Her first academic appointment was at Wake Forest University in North Carolina but she still doesn't understand basketball or American football at all. Her favorite deadly sin is greed.

Connolly is currently Associate Professor of Contemporary Poetry at the University of Houston. Her debut book *Grief and Meter: Elegies for Poets After Auden* is the first to consider that specific sub-genre of elegy and was published by the University of Virginia Press in 2016. She is currently working on a book about the poetry of the AIDS epidemic. Her articles and reviews can be found in publications such as *Poetry, The Times Literary Supplement, Literary Imagination, Yeats Annual, Plume* and the *London Evening Standard*.

www.ingramcontent.com/pod-product-compliance
Lightning Source LLC
Chambersburg PA
CBHW020330170426
43200CB00006B/330